Praise for *Rob Bell and a New Ame*

Twenty years from now we may look back on Rob Bell as the man who forever changed the face of American evangelical Christianity. Thank God, then, for James Wellman's profile of this complex, controversial, and utterly compelling religious leader. This is a book that should be read by all Americans regardless of their religious affiliation.

—Reza Aslan, author of *No god but God*
and *Beyond Fundamentalism*

Rob Bell is a phenomenon. The emotional outpouring evidenced in both his critics and supporters demonstrate that his work has isolated and exposed a crises within that exists within the Evangelical community. A crisis that, once brought to the surface, has the potential of short circuiting fundamentalist strains within the movement and clearing the path for a theological reformation. This book is among the first to provide an insight into the development of Bell's thought and chart the significance of his intervention in the rocky landscape of Christian culture.

—Peter Rollins, author of *How (Not) to Speak of God*
and *Insurrection: To Believe Is Human To Doubt is Divine*

Much more than a biography, Wellman uses the life of Rob Bell to reveal the inner logic of a growing orthodoxy in American Christianity. Wellman traces the maturing of this charismatic preacher from an earnest young pastor to a nuanced bestselling "heretic"—and in doing so maps the development of a more ambiguous, more open evangelicalism. This remarkably readable study of Bell's ministry illuminates the controversies, connects the histories, and explains the theologies. As the most public figure manifesting the transformation of American evangelicalism, Bell's less dogmatic, more relational faith may hold the key to its sustainable future. Even those familiar with his ministry will find new insights and come away with a deeper sense of Rob Bell's intimate connection to the developing history of modern Christianity.

—Gerardo Marti, L. Richardson King Associate Professor
of Sociology at Davidson College, and author of
A Mosaic of Believers and Hollywood Faith

rob Bell and
a *new* American Christianity

JAMES K WELLMAN JR

Abingdon Press
Nashville

No part of this work may be reproduced or transmitted in any form or by any means, electronic or mechanical, including photocopying and recording, or by any information storage or retrieval system, except as may be expressly permitted by the 1976 Copyright Act or in writing from the publisher. Requests for permission can be addressed to Permissions, The United Methodist Publishing House, P.O. Box 801, 201 Eighth Avenue South, Nashville, TN 37202-0801, or e-mailed to permissions@umpublishing.org.

All scripture quotations unless noted otherwise are taken from the New International Version, © 2010. Used by permission. All rights reserved.

Scripture quotations marked CEB are from the Common English Bible, © 2011. Used by permission. All rights reserved.

Scripture quotations marked ESV are from the English Standard Version, © 2001. Used by permission. All rights reserved.

Library of Congress Cataloging-in-Publication Data

Wellman, James K.
   Rob Bell and a new American Christianity / by James K. Wellman, Jr.
      pages cm
   Includes bibliographical references and index.
      ISBN 978-1-4267-4844-8 (book - pbk. / trade pbk. : alk. paper) 1. Bell, Rob.
2. Evangelists—United States—Biography. 3. Christianity—United States—21st
century. 4. Christianity and culture—United States—History—21st century. I. Title.
   BV3785.B416W45 2012
   269'.2092—dc23
   [B]
                                        2012030118

This book is printed on acid-free paper.

12 13 14 15 16 17 18 19 20 21—10 9 8 7 6 5 4 3 2 1
MANUFACTURED IN THE UNITED STATES OF AMERICA

For Billy and Beast, brothers in the spirit, always.

CONTENTS

MYSTERY

Rob Bell's star is rising, even as he remains (and loves remaining) a man of mystery. His person and work provoke visceral reactions that range from adoration to repulsion, while raising profound questions. In 2011 he was named to the *Time* 100 list—the 100 most influential people in the world. That same year, Bell left Mars Hill, a megachurch, which he founded in 1999, to pursue broader opportunities in Hollywood to, as he explained, "compellingly share the gospel."

Bell is known to many for his *Nooma* films, a series of twenty-four, twelve-minute sermons. At the time of this writing, these films have been downloaded nearly three million times. In 2001 Bell switched publishing houses to HarperOne and hit the New York Times bestseller list with his controversial book, titled *Love Wins: A Book about Heaven, Hell, and the Fate of Every Person Who Ever Lived.*

In 2012, Bell worked on a hybrid talk show featuring religious *and* spiritual content—including interviews, short sermon-like presentations, and world-changing ideas—collected from Bell's tenure at Mars Hill. It was a show that Bell insisted had "never been done before." This show was developed after the TV show *Stronger*—which was based on Bell's unpublished novel—failed to be piloted by the Studios, despite being produced by *Lost's* Carlton Cuse.

So, who is Rob Bell? As a pastor and an artist, Bell exhibits the irrepressible spirit of the American religious entrepreneur, but his story also serves as a frame to explore deeper patterns within the seismic shifts in modern American culture. His story and life function as a leading indicator of what it means to be a Christian in the changing modern American religious landscape.

The face of American Christianity is in transition, and Rob Bell, with his own evolving look and artistry, has opened a window on this hybrid horizon.

By hailing from a conservative Christian background, Bell has maintained the core attribute of the faith—a passion for Jesus—but has also built a career and a philosophy of life that is more complex than what we usually attribute to American evangelical circles. For much of his pastoral career he has been a superstar in the evangelical world, but his appeal is much broader, including the "spiritual but not religious," liberal Christians across the spectrum, and even folks who simply admire his artistry as a communicator.

Of course, not all consumers of Bell's work are equally enthused. Evangelicals frequently discount Bell's efforts as "fluff," and "pabulum," consumed by unknowing and uneducated young people. One evangelical pastor told me, "He is one of the most dangerous figures on the Christian landscape today."[1] Still others in evangelical circles have dismissed him as a heretic or worse.

Mark Driscoll, the equally controversial and popular evangelical pastor, who planted a church called Mars Hill just a year before Bell's, rails against Bell as some sort of biblical heretic: "I don't know him; he's a creative guy and an amazing communicator, but he holds up rabbinical authority as a key to Bible interpretation. If a Rabbi doesn't love Jesus, they have a bad interpretation. Bell argues that the Bible sets into motion a direction that while it appears to contradict the Bible literally, we should nonetheless embrace it. This came out

---

1 Quote from a conversation with the author, from an evangelical pastor, who requested anonymity.

when he shifted from male elders on his board to female elders. It's not biblical."[2] Bell is well-known for using various forms of media to circulate his view of Christianity. He makes his teachings easily accessible through new mediums, including film, while concurrently never shrinking from complicated discussions. In the 2007 film, *Everything is Spiritual,* he describes the evolutionary story of creation, mixing a dense but clear explication of the scientific origins of the universe, all framed within a wider worldview that humans, by nature, are spiritual—there is nothing humans do that is not spiritual.

A friend of mine who stands outside of Christianity but has deep interests in religion and spirituality viewed Bell's film. Though admiring his intelligence and artfulness, he exclaimed in frustration, "Why is Bell so determined to retrieve Christianity? He's obviously a very smart guy and he gets the science of creation and its spiritual corollary, but why force it into the Christian narrative?"

In fact, what makes Bell's voice so unique is that he *is* willing to use every medium and discipline to convey that the Christian story is by its very nature fundamental to every aspect of life, regardless of what others might think, or how interpreters, whether religious or not, might react.

Bell's recognition and celebrity hit a new high with the publication of *Love Wins*—a 2011 New York Times bestseller. The book and the controversy skyrocketed Bell into the national media. In *Love Wins,* Bell invoked the well-known interpretation of the kingdom of God, which holds that heaven *and* hell may not be somewhere else—but that, rather, they are right here among us. For Bell, the "new creation" in Christ is already working within creation to transform it through the death and resurrection of Jesus Christ.

---

2 A talk given by Mark Driscoll on March 7, 2009, in which he critiques the emergent church movement, and Rob Bell in particular. http://videorow.blogspot.com/2009/03/mark-driscoll-critiques-rob-bell-and.html. Accessed December 1, 2011.

This is hardly a new idea, but Bell's placement within the evangelical community, created a firestorm even as it drew the interest not only of many young evangelicals, but also of readers across the religious and ideological spectrum.

Nonetheless, the voices of young Calvinist evangelical leaders condemned *Love Wins* with a comprehensive and ferocious attack. Pastor and author Kevin DeYoung called Bell's Christology "classic liberalism," his use of scripture "mistaken" and a form of "biblicism," his history "misleading," and his eschatology "muddled," finally concluding that Bell is a "universalist" who worships "a different god . . . [a] small god so bound by notions of radical free will that I wonder how Bell can be so confident God's love will melt the hardest heart."[3]

The fierce nature of these attacks is balanced by the passionate tone of positive responses to Bell. For many he is a celebrity and a rock star. In one short YouTube video, a random Mars Hill attendee says she wants to meet Rob Bell, and her friend responds, "Let's go now." The college student and friend go, meeting Bell on the stage at Mars Hill where the three of them talk. Afterward Bell gives each of them an awkward but gentle hug around the shoulders, his face maintaining a calm and pastoral look. When the video shifts to their return from meeting Bell, the girl exclaims, "Why am I acting like this is a celebrity?"[4] But she isn't alone in viewing Bell as a celebrity. A friend of Bell's told me that he was recently walking with Bell in New York City when a group of young women ran up to Bell to ask for autographs.

I had an even more personal experience with this phenomenon. During the course of my research, my fifteen-year-old daughter got to know Rob Bell through the *Nooma* films. Soon after I started this project, the complete set of *Nooma* DVDs came in the mail, and my

---

3 See Kevin DeYoung's blog, "God is Still Holy and what you learned in Sunday school is Still True: A Review of Love Wins by Rob Bell." March 14, 2011. http://thegospelcoalition.org/blogs/kevindeyoung/2011/03/14/rob-bell-love-wins-review/. Accessed November 30, 2012.

4 See the short YouTube clip at: http://www.youtube.com/watch?v=xmMp1Sv1FXo. Accessed December 17, 2011.

daughter suggested we do a father/daughter night and start watching them together. She bubbled, "I like him better in brown hair" (referring to his blond stage in the earliest films). In the later films, when Bell is pictured with a crew cut, she exclaimed, "I like him better with long hair!" After we watched the fourth film, she murmured, "I love Rob Bell," then moving past the hair comments, she added, "I feel like he understands where I'm coming from; I want to be like him."

This kind of adoration is exhibited not only by young people, but also by a legion of older followers who see him as a gifted communicator of a message that moved them. One online reviewer described Bell's *Drop Like the Stars* Tour Film on Amazon: "The idea that a person could essentially preach a two hour sermon, hold the attention of those participating the entire time, make people laugh, make people cry, have them do something during the interaction that not only heals those who are present, but also does some good for a group of people in need, and then records it so that other people can witness what happened during a two hour gathering is ludicrous. And yet, Bell doesn't even look like he's trying. He pulls it off with the same grace and humility we have come to expect from him."[5]

A thirty-year-old volunteer at Mars Hill who had tried out different churches explained her experience to me like this: "I was looking for a form of Christianity that is real, gritty, and matches the experience of my life—and I found what I was looking for here. We talk about the issues that we all face here and how faith makes a difference; it's real, it's powerful and it gives me hope for the church."[6]

These powerful reactions to Bell don't come only from his own "tribe" of evangelicals. A progressive Episcopalian priest who has one of the fastest-growing churches in his diocese explained, "I was searching for some good, honest, progressive media to use with

---

5 See this review at: http://www.amazon.com/Drops-Like-Stars-Tour-Film/product-reviews/0310671345. Accessed January 15, 2012.

6 Personal communication with the author on a visit to Mars Hill Bible Church, November 20. 2011.

adolescents as we tried to forge a spirituality of sexuality. I found one of his short films—from his *Nooma* series—where he talks about sex, the Bible, his own passions, and then pours gasoline on a pile of old timber the size of a house and strikes a match. I came to see that Rob had a pastor's heart of compassion, and an incisive mind that seemed hungry to search beyond the first answer to the questions he was asking. Still, here's the best part: the kids in my high school youth group, when they saw that first Bell film, they 'got it.' "[7]

The love, devotion, and controversy that Rob Bell evokes shows from the sales of his books and films, and also from the popularity of his sermon podcasts (with 40,000 to 55,000 downloads per week while at Mars Hill). Bell strikes a chord.

What makes Bell so attractive? Many pastors and leaders want to create this kind of devotion. Some of the criticism of Bell is based, at least in part, on envy of his ability to attract an audience. What is this "charismatic bond" between Bell and his listeners?[8]

While attendees of megachurches often say that the pastor is not the reason they attend,[9] there is little doubt that these "energy stars" attract and create a fusion of joy, delight, and motivation that create congregations that glow with what they call the "spirit" of God.[10] My interest in the work of Rob Bell stemmed from my work as a sociologist; I know that skilled leaders generate a collective effervescence that buoys groups and charges crowds with a kind of delirium that humans want—and even need. This can happen in any group, but not every leader can produce this kind of multisensory mélange of input that is often called the "feeling of the spirit of God," or "the

---

7 Personal communication with the author, October 20, 2011.

8 See Douglas Madsen's and Peter G. Snow's, *The Charismatic Bond: Political Behavior in the Time of Crisis.* Cambridge, MA: Harvard University Press, 1991.

9 In this midst of writing this book, I was analyzing a survey of twelve national megachurches for my next book entitled *High on God: How the Megachurch Conquered America.* NY: Oxford University Press, forthcoming in 2013.

10 "Energy star," comes from Randall Collins' *Interaction Ritual Chains.* Princeton, NJ: Princeton University Press, 2004. Energy stars are those who attract a following and evoke emotional energy from others.

touch of God." Whatever language you use to describe it, I've seen it lift people out of their seats.

Despite his popularity, Bell's rock star persona repulses many people. Outsiders, particularly those from non-religious backgrounds, find it manipulative or dangerous. Others, including those in the evangelical community, and particularly in response to *Love Wins*, have thrown him overboard. John Piper, the godfather of the neo-Reformed movement in American evangelical Christianity, tweeted, "Farewell Rob Bell," which he later said was meant as a friendly remark. Albert Mohler, president of the Southern Baptist Theological Seminary, called Bell's views on hell an "unscriptural sentimentalism . . . incompatible with [God's] hatred of sin."[11] And book after book have detailed Bell's heretical ways.

So, is Rob Bell a heretic? Does this question even make sense in an American culture that has so many kinds of Christianity?[12] Just what kind of Christian is he? Whatever one thinks of Rob Bell, there is no denying the intense controversy surrounding him in the American religious landscape—and that these contentions raise important questions for multiple audiences:

Should evangelicals be afraid of him?

Should young Reformed evangelicals see him as their mentor?

Should pastors, of whatever label, take him as a model?

Should the spiritual but not religious see him as a kind of spiritual avatar?

The onrush of responses to his work indicates that many see him as a voice of faith. Increasing numbers of evangelicals, particularly young evangelicals, are asking questions about the faith. They are questioning the exclusive claims of Christianity and hoping for a

---

11 See Albert Mohler's blog, "Doing Away with Hell? Part One." March 8, 2011. http://www.albertmohler.com/2011/03/08/doing-away-with-hell-part-one/. Accessed December 2, 2011.

12 See Mark Silk's and Andrew Walsh's, *One Nation, Divisible: How Regional Religious Differences Shape American Politics*. Lanham, MD: Rowman & Littlefield Publishers, Inc., 2008. Silk and Walsh provide empirical verification to show the powerful religious and political hybridity of American Christianity.

more fruitful relationship with cultures outside the faith community; they want answers to their toughest questions.[13]

One of the most fascinating questions that this book will explore is the degree and depth of Bell's influence on the American Christian community. As a scholar of American religion, I believe that the decline and even the end of the Protestant establishment is an inevitable outcome of our religious history. The Protestant mainline is no longer mainline; establishment Protestantism simply doesn't attract a large audience any more. The evangelical networks don't fare much better. It, too, is fragmented, and some argue that we've seen the "End of Evangelicalism."[14] The center of American Christianity no longer holds, if it ever did. Is Bell's work and person catalyzing a new kind of American Christianity? And what are the contours of this new form?

An Evangelical Artist

Rob Bell's story has many layers, and Bell's ability as a performer and an artist is a critical aspect to his communication and leadership style. Bell's creativity, audacity, and perseverance powered the founding of the Mars Hill church. The story of its "founding" is legendary—the first Sunday, 500 chairs were set up, and more than 1,000 people showed up. Many now describe the church as a 10,000-member congregation—though the number of attendees varies dramatically. On one visit in 2011, at one of Bell's final sermons at Mars Hill, I noted more than a total of 6,000 attendees at the two services; both worship services were nearly filled.

---

13 See David Kinnaman's *You Lost Me: Why Young Christians are Leaving Church and Rethinking the Faith.* Grand Rapids, MI: Baker Books, 2011. Kinnaman gives six typical reasons for why young Christians are leaving the church: churches are overprotective; shallow; anti-science; simplistic about sexuality; exclusivistic, and unfriendly to doubt.

14 See David Fitch's provocative *The End of Evangelicalism: Discerning a New Faithfulness for Mission: Towards an Evangelical Political Theology.* Eugene, OR: Cascade Books, 2011.

For more than ten years, Bell built a hybrid institution—part cathedral to his own genius (and some would say ego) and part workshop for experimentation. It became a canvas for him as an artist in a new kind of church. Few resources were spent on the building infrastructure itself; nearly everything was invested in the message, music, and mission of the church.

Bell's original mission statement—tongue in cheek—repeated the following words for ten pages, "Disciples who make disciples, who make disciples, who make disciples." Bell reiterated the same motto in 2009, a simple, direct, unadulterated appeal to follow Jesus.

One of the ironies in this story is that Bell's canvas, Mars Hill church, occupies a drab, old mall—a fact that Bell loved to reference in his sermons there, playing off the juxtaposition of sacred space and the perfume bars that preceded it. With Bell at the helm, church members created a sanctuary in the space that had housed the defunct mall's anchor store. This sanctuary is now able to seat 3,500 people. In the middle of the room is the stage, and above it is a series of large, four sided screens, easily accessible to viewing from all sides. The walls, painted battleship grey, are clean and sober. The commercial feel of the strip mall and its ultra-secularity underscores the bold power of the claim that the sacred insinuates itself in all places and at all times. How and why Bell stayed at the mall and never chose to build a worship center is central to this story, a fact that I explore later in the volume. It is important to how Bell chose to strategize the growth of his church and is also deeply embedded in his own philosophical understanding of life in God and in faith.

Similarly, the Mars Hill website is cold and precise, though it enchants with its graphically delicate, sophisticated, and postmodern presentation. It communicates the message: "Yes, we want your eyes and your interest, but it's okay not to enter." There is a sort of "come-hither" feel with a touch of detachment. And this same sense reverberates throughout Bell's presentations and expressions: "Yes, we want you and we love you, but we aren't desperate, and if this doesn't work for you, it's okay." And true to this style, as the story shows,

Bell made changes and preached sermons in response to which he lost thousands of attendees on several occasions.

Bell's mantra of a "non-anxious state" bubbles up in many of his sermons—announcing that the goal of Christian transformation is the art of being one's self, a peaceful presence, with the ultimate purpose of "entrusting oneself to God." This power of a peaceful presence provokes and appeals to a young, postmodern aesthetic, and that's exactly the point. Young people can smell manipulation. And Bell's confident, deprecating, and even goofy style diffuses this concern.

Bell's talent is also found in the hybrid nature of his work—using state of the art media to communicate his gospel in clever forms. The *Nooma* videos, the first of which was filmed on 9/11, not only elevated an emerging genre (dramatic video vignettes were in use during worship and in teaching at several megachurches through the mid 1990s) but also shifted the tone and character of how pastors present themselves. Much of what is seen as "hip" Christian media is now a direct spinoff of Bell's work. The initial distributor whom Bell approached about the project scoffed at the idea that it would sell: "You can't just invent a new genre." The story of the beginning and ending of *Nooma* communicates much about Bell and his ability to tap talent in ways that produced what many call a "bit of genius." All of this despite the fact that Bell's relationship with Flannel, the nonprofit that produced the series, ended badly.

In the midst of his success with the *Nooma* videos, Bell took his act on tour. He went to secular outlets in cities across the country and the world. His movies include a handful of tour films, each based on his itinerant lectures. Bell's innovation is a combination of storytelling and sermonizing that arises directly from a restless creativity that pushes him to make things, expressing ideas that, as he exclaims, "are bursting up from within." Bell's creative drive is part and parcel of who he is and what his faith is about. What began as a form of chutzpah (the *Nooma* series and his tour films) and turned into new adventures with his TV ambitions. In all of this Bell exemplifies a certain fearlessness combined with the talent to invent whole new ways of communicating his message.

This vision to "compellingly share the gospel," in words and language that people outside of churches can understand, is what motivates him. And even this language is complex. What does Bell mean by "the gospel?" For him this "gospel" is a penetrating form of good news that he is passionate to share. As he often proclaims in sermons, "We are a people who believe the tomb is empty; we are a resurrection people." For him this means everything—that is, the very warp and woof of reality communicates this movement from crucifixion to resurrection, death to new life. In this sense, despite some conservative Christians' critiques of him, he is genuinely passionate that the life, death, and resurrection of Jesus Christ tell a new story. And this story is the one with which he wants to "evangelize."

Some have compared him to Billy Graham. And, to be sure, the itinerant and unabashed nature of his communication makes the comparison apt. At the end of every sermon there is some sort of call or challenge, although this is not often a direct invitation to accept Christ but most frequently a call to transformation. And so we ask, does Bell want to convert folks? Or is he telling a story that invites people into a spiritual journey that they are already on? Most Americans don't want to be converted, nor do they believe they need to be. Many feel that they are already "spiritual." Bell asks questions that he believes few people are asking, and then he invites his audience to come on the journey and discover, for themselves, what he has found.

Bell's move to Los Angeles underscores the spirit of his journey. LA is the fount of the "spiritual but not religious" movement in America, and Bell dovetails with this tradition in key ways.[15] Bell's emphasis

---

15 See Catherine Albanese's *The Republic of the Mind: A Cultural History of American Metaphysical Religion.* New Haven, CT: Yale University Press, 2008. Albanese describes this metaphysical religion as a "combinative nature"—preoccupied with mind and powers; tying itself to ancient sources; focusing on movement and energy, and looking for salvation as comfort, therapy, and healing.

on story as the good news' vehicle attracts and tantalizes many both inside and outside of evangelical circles. His relentless critique of religion and its forms appeals to many who are a part of this "spiritual but not religious" movement, but for him, the story *is at its heart* about Jesus and his death and resurrection. As he explained to me, "Some stories are better than others." For Bell, there is *the* story—the Jesus story, which is deeply spiritual and transformative of human consciousness. Religious forms, per se, don't matter to him, but the content of the story—Jesus—matters and remains.

Bell's attempt to make it in television marks the innovation of something quite new. And the natural question is how will this change his identity? Will he become a kind of cult of personality, or as some would say, a further extension of the cult that he has already created? Predecessors within the Christian tradition have faced similar prospects and the temptations are real, but so are the opportunities—and this tension is precisely what intrigues so many.

Bell's own story, his inner drama and failings, deeply impact this trajectory. The introspective nature of his work and his personal use of psychological counseling underscore his own struggles to understand himself. The story of his early life and his family's influence deeply impact how he relates to the world, his take on the Christian faith, his vocation as an artist, and his early tendency to subvert conventions and obligations that he found either silly or boring. The roots of this active and hybrid nature and how they translate and express his faith are a critical aspect of this story, essential for understanding the cultural context of how he came to be and what he made of it.

Bell and the American Religious Revolution

American Christianity is changing. Polls show that 70 percent of Americans believe there are multiple forms of religion that can get people to heaven. This is a *huge* shift from the early twentieth century. In 1924, 91 percent of Americans believed that Christianity was the only true religion; today, only 41 percent do.[16] Bell's ideas are both controversial and appealing in the minds and hearts of many listeners and readers. To progressives, it reaffirms what they already believe. For evangelicals, there's a mixed reaction: to the younger evangelical generation it's part temptation, part seduction; to older evangelicals, particularly self-identified conservative Christians, it's heresy. Tearing down walls and questioning older forms is Bell's *forte*, done with a smile and a kind of cooing delight that tantalizes, and draws people in.

Bell is nothing but ambitious. As he explained to me, "Why not swing for the fences?" He believes Jesus' teachings have the potential to break down barriers between Christians and all other faiths—a challenge with ramifications for the parochial concerns of individual Christian denominations as well as the sustainability of global religious cultures.

Bell's relation to religion and politics is even more complex. Raised in a staunch conservative and Reagan Republican household, he graduated from Wheaton College and was a card-carrying evangelical. He spent his early years in a conservative church in Grand Rapids, the seat of Reformed evangelicalism. As such, Bell lived in the furnace of evangelical piety, so his transformation and eventual move away from this setting is fraught with its own complications. The reasons for the move tell us a great deal about who he is and perhaps what is happening within the American Christian evangelical culture. And this is important since statistically, if 50 to 75 million American adults identify as evangelicals, even if not all have a Reformed theology, then this group can make a claim to be *the* new American Christian mainstream.[17]

---

16 See Mark Chaves' *American Religion: Contemporary Trends*. Princeton, NJ: Princeton University Press, 2011.

17 See my *Evangelicals vs. Liberals: The Clash of Christian Cultures in the Pacific Northwest*. NY: Oxford University Press, 2008. For statistics about how Americans

Christian history is a minefield of misadventures in religious politics, and American religion has its own unique story.[18] The challenge that American evangelicalism currently faces is the schizoid nature of its adherents. Even one or two generations ago, evangelicals were sectarian and staunchly against any participation in American politics. Today, American evangelicals are one of the major forces in the Republican Party.[19]

Billy Graham, more than any other figure, expressed and facilitated the movement of fundamentalist Christianity into the mainstream. Graham hobnobbed with presidents even as he preached his message of "repent and be saved," arguing that, without Christ, people were damned. Now, even some within the evangelical camp are questioning not only the exclusive claims of conservative Christianity but also the very heart of the evangelical belief that the Bible is inerrant.[20]

The twentieth-century claim of inerrancy is a legacy of the Reformation's *sola scriptura*—the idea that all one needs for salvation can be found in the Bible. Today, this idea is reinforced by the claim that the scriptures of the Old and New Testaments are complete, and entirely without error. While Bell subscribes to the authority of scripture, he

---

self-identify, see Barry A. Kosmin, Egon Mayer and Ariela Keysar. *American Religious Identification Survey.* NY: The Graduate Center of the City University of New York, 2001.

18 See my article, written with S.R. Thompson, that gives a history of American Christianity and U.S. foreign policy, "From the Social Gospel to Neoconservativism: Religion and U.S. Foreign Policy." *Interdisciplinary Journal of Research on Religion.* Volume 7, Article 6: pp. 1-41. http://www.religjournal.com/

19 Aimee Semple McPherson is one of the most fascinating exceptions to this trend; she set a precedent for the Christian Right, building Angelus Temple in 1923 in Los Angeles and developing a Christian patriotism with flag and Bible in each hand. See Matthew Sutton's biography, *Aimee Semple McPherson and the Resurrection of Christian America.* Cambridge, MA: Harvard University Press, 2007.

20 See Christian Smith's recent devastating attack on biblicism and inerrancy, *The Bible Made Impossible: Why Biblicism is Not a Truly Evangelical Reading of the Bible.* Grand Rapids, MI: Brazos Press, 2011. Smith, a professor of sociology at the University of Notre Dame, embodies all of these shifts; he went to an evangelical college and was one himself, but has recently converted to Roman Catholicism.

veers away from these exacting terms. He most often talks about the story of faith—noting that faith is far more about the action of the story and the way in which the biblical story can transform one's own. The rise of biblical inerrancy was a function of the fundamentalist movement of the last century. Fundamentalism rejected the liberalism of modernity and defended the scriptures as the axis point upon which faith could be built. Fundamentalist colleges swelled in size in the 1960s and 1970s. Jerry Falwell, along with many others, politicized the movement in the 1980s and 1990s with potent consequences in the elections of Ronald Reagan and George W. Bush, but even as Falwell Christianized the Republican Party, he didn't achieve the moral majority that he sought.

The election of Barack Obama, the growing movement to legalize gay marriage, the end of "Don't ask, Don't tell," the continuing legality of abortion, and the growing "no religion" movement in American life have thrown much of the Christian Right into a reevaluation of its place in politics and culture.

Bell's actions must be seen within the context of a generation trying to find new ways to live out a Christian life in face of the fact that fundamentalism, as a movement, has lost much of its vitality. The failure of fundamentalism to create a sustainable political culture, and its tendency to cause many to reject Christianity, have fostered a younger generation that looks for less militant ways to be Christian and strives to live out beliefs beyond unilateral political demands.

How has Bell negotiated these turbulent waters? His book *Jesus Wants to Save Christians* and his brief move with his family into a Grand Rapids slum in 2008 and 2009 catapulted him in the direction of social justice, a form of radical politics, and a kind of liberation theology. But this, too, was an experiment, a part of his sometimes impulsive attempt to live into his thought and be found true to his word: noble in that sense, but in the end unworkable for him and his family.

A potent and consistent theme of Bell's ministry has been an empathy and solidarity with those on the margins, and it is this theme that is deep within his psyche. Bell's early stories recount how his mom saw in him sympathy for hurting people. Bell's own brush with death, contracting meningitis in his last year of college, and a potent and visceral identification with people who struggle, dominate the rhetoric and tone of most, if not all, of his sermons.

This sympathy for the excluded and marginalized is striking, particularly as it runs parallel with his fascination with the power of media and his desire to perform in ever-larger venues. His flirtation with the "big time," began early in his pastoral career when representatives from Hollywood approached him on several occasions. It's difficult to relate to the margins when you're simultaneously at the center of media power.

This tension is not lost on him. The dalliance and distance between Christianity and power has been a part of the Christian heritage nearly from its beginning. Bell's temptations are a part of an old story, and Bell's enticements have been epic. The story of this negotiation and its methods are some of the most fascinating aspects of this remarkable American life.

Prophet of a New American Christianity?

Bell's timing is right. Over the last century, American culture has shifted from one that was thoroughly infused by the Christian faith to one that freely expresses multiple perspectives on faith and spirituality. In American Christian culture, subdivisions multiply at a meteoric rate. Religion in general, and particularly the Christian faith, is up for grabs. Most Americans no longer believe there is only one way to eternal life. The culture is an open religious market.

Bell lives this reality and glories in the free market of choice. In response to his critics who called him a heretic after the publication of *Love Wins,* Bell responded with a note of defiance, "'Everybody is forced to believe or think or subscribe to a particular thing, but there are those who are able to choose—how awesome is that?' [Bell] even embraces being called a heretic—identifying the word's etymological roots 'in a Greek word *hairetikos,* meaning 'able to choose.' Laughing as he said, 'One of the most lethal aspects of that word—heretic—is that it ends discussions, rather than starts them.' Turning more serious, Bell warns, 'And that's why I think it's so dangerous. It ends discussion, and it's holding hands with violence.' "[21]

Bell's audacity is buoyed by a culture that allows bold and restless questions to be asked, and a Christian culture that has lost its ability to quiet dissenters. The history of American Christianity is full of heresy trials, and Christian innovators have frequently lost their positions and been judged as cranks or worse. Experimenters and innovators have also thrived—Aimee Semple McPherson, despite the rumors of her sexual dalliances, maintained a following similar to Bell's. Billy Graham honed his world circuit, preaching an Old Time Gospel of salvation from sin through Christ, all the while benefitting from his closeness to American political power, which gave him unparalleled access to global cultures. Not unlike McPherson and Graham, Bell carries a restless energy that refuses to bow to convention and is ambitious to carve out new creative outlets for his work.

Important evangelical voices argue that Bell is birthing a type of Christian renaissance: Greg Boyd, an evangelical pastor and author of *The Myth of a Christian Nation,* baptized Bell's book *Love Wins* calling it "a bold, prophetic, and poetic masterpiece." Eugene Peterson, arguably the most respected American evangelical pastor, also testified to Bell's importance: "It isn't easy to develop a biblical imagination that takes in the comprehensive and eternal work of Christ . . . Rob Bell goes a long way in helping us acquire just such an imagination—without a trace of the soft sentimentality and without compromising an inch of evangelical conviction."

Hints of Bell's importance and influence are everywhere, but perhaps one of the most telling is actually on the back cover of *Love Wins.* One of the publicity blurbs is a quote taken from Andrew Crouch, an editor for Christianity Today: "Rob Bell is a central figure for his

---

21 This conversation is quoted from an interview with Cathleen Falsani, "The Heretical Rob Bell and Why Love Wins," March 14, 2011. See http://www.huffingtonpost.com/cathleen-falsani/rob-bell-heretic-schmeret_b_835606.html. Accessed November 28, 2011.

generation and for the way that evangelicals are likely to do church in the next twenty years."[22] Crouch never endorsed *Love Wins,* and even as his personal estimation of Bell remains high, Crouch's assessment of Bell's influence has decreased. In part, Crouch's estimation is the result of Bell's movement away from institutional leadership, and his observation seems to echo Bell's own ambivalence about being a social movement leader. Indeed Bell's complex impulses and flirtations with leadership are a large part of the broader story of this book.

And so while accolades pile up, the test of any achievement is its results. Bell's revolution may turn out to be a moment of true change, but it could also be nothing more than a masterpiece to his own charged imagination.

Even as Bell innovates, his passion is to communicate the gospel of Jesus Christ. Of course, this phrase the "gospel of Jesus Christ," has meant many things to many people. For Bell, there is an insistent theme and deep love for what he describes as the "brilliance of Jesus." His sermons, which I take as his most potent and powerful communicative genre, tumble over with scriptural references, pointing to a gospel dominated by the figure of Jesus and his transformative message of good news. Faith, as he says, is to be "awake." It is to recognize and "to see" the form of the divine love that is incarnating itself in and through the creation.

Bell claims that this universal process of progressive incarnation finds its fulfillment in Jesus Christ. While the process of incarnation is stalled by human sin, it is not stopped. It culminates in the death and resurrection of Jesus Christ, whereby Christ reconciles all things to God. The power of the restoration of all things has no limit and works not only on the human body and soul but also into the very roots of the creation itself. For Bell, heaven is not somewhere else— God redeems and transforms the earth, where God dwells among his people.

---

22 See John Leland's "Center Stage for a Pastor Where It's Rock that Usually Rules." *The New York Times,* July 8, 2006. http://www.nytimes.com/2006/07/08/us/08minister.html?_r=1.

Bell's gospel message is remarkably different than that heard from most evangelical pulpits. The more traditional American evangelical message speaks of the reality of human sin and the need to be saved by the blood of Christ—both to avoid hell and to win heaven. And while Bell doesn't go out of the way to argue that they are wrong, he does suggest it, allowing the reader and hearer to make up their own minds. His own relationship with the camp has become more and more precarious. He avoids naming enemies or identifying himself by who he is against, but he maintains points of differentiation in his theology and philosophy of faith that dance at the very edges of acceptable evangelical dogma.

Bell brings innovations to the way he communicates and re-thinks the faith. Unlike many in evangelical spheres, he is informed by an artistic and aesthetic sensibility that makes use of story and sees the art of story as *the instrument* of faith. Many misunderstand his commitment to the arts, not just as a tool of expression, but also as a pathway of faith itself. The arts, for him, are a deeply subversive act in the world, and Jesus, in this sense, is the great artist who flummoxes his followers and turns their worlds upside down—aesthetically, morally, and religiously.

Bell's narrative-based theology affirms science, sees the universe as an expression of God's creative act in Christ, and makes the claim that God in Christ is reconciling "all things" to God. What makes Bell fascinating is that he communicates all of this with the passion of an evangelical preacher. His theology and approach strike at the heart of evangelical theology and appeal to many who are trying to integrate faith into a world that is becoming ever larger and more pluralistic, both culturally and religiously.

Bell's Radical Claim

Religious pluralism is a crucial issue to understand when considering Bell's place on the American religious landscape. Many people, whether conservative or liberal, wonder why they should stay with Christianity. For those inside the Christian fold, the question arises—can a person maintain faith *and* see truth in other traditions? Because the faith has been so denigrated by its secular critics, many Christians wonder if Christianity has an intellectual leg to stand on. Many younger evangelicals who have grown up in anti-science sub-cultures wonder if the faith is sturdy enough to live in a world of real, alternative worldviews.

But for Bell, the sacred is in the secular, and the two cannot be separated.

Many interpreters of Bell miss this radical claim. Some see him as "sold out" to hip culture, others as a "spiritual but not religious" lightweight. Pulling back the layers, however, Bell's picture synthesizes a Christocentric worldview, through which and out of which Bell *shows,* rather than explains, that God "was definitely in this place and I didn't know it" (CEB, Gen 28:16, one of his favorite verses).

Others claim, "He simply uses secular language as a Trojan Horse to slip in a Christian message, why should I be manipulated in this way?" Martin Beshir, for example, in a controversial NBC television interview about *Love Wins,* accused Bell of "amending the gospel" to appeal to a popular audience.[23]

Yet, part of this is the complexity of his message which Bell attempts to work into multiple cultural frames, for example slipping a Christian message into secular culture, translating secular thought into Christianity, planting a liberal Christian message into evangelicalism, and taking the passion of the evangelical message into liberal Christianity. His interpreters, admirers, and critics hold myriads of perspectives, apparently in conflict, that all apply to Bell. This is part of what makes him such an intriguing person.

This book is an evaluation of the story of Rob Bell and what it means for the future of faith in America. It is an evaluation of his message, his person, his theology, and the ever-evolving important questions he asks himself, others, and the church.

---

23 Footage from this interview can be found here: http://www.youtube.com/watch?v=Vg-qgmJ7nzA. Accessed January 15, 2012.

chapter two

SUBVERSION

"These figures, representing the poor and the deformed,
appear to symbolize the moral values of communitas as against the
coercive power of supreme political rulers."

Victor Turner, The Ritual Process: Structure and Anti-Structure, p 110.

On one level, it's strange to call Rob Bell subversive or label him as some kind of outsider. After all, he is a best-selling author, mega-church pastor, filmmaker, and TV producer. And yet, his role as an outsider is one the central themes of this book.

Bell is a celebrity, yet he claims to identify with "the poor and the deformed." Though he may be considered a media star, he continues to speak with empathy for those who are the "zeroes," the ones "in the back row."

And at the heart of the story of Rob Bell is a tale of a kid who didn't fit in, who felt like he failed to read the "secret guidebook" to the successful life. This theme of subverting the system, even as he triumphs in it, runs through his early childhood, his college years, and even his ministry at Mars Hill. It was through his experiences of being an outsider that Bell learned to look at the world with different eyes and created a life and ministry from a vision honed by hours contemplating ways to upend entrenched views about the world, the church, the Christian faith and himself.

Tony Jones, one of the leaders of the emergent church movement—an evangelical subculture translating the gospel using the language and aesthetics of secular culture—explains this strange mixture of Bell's traits that led him to become a star. In early 2011, Jones predicted, with perfect pitch, what would happen with Bell as a result of his release of the controversial bestseller *Love Wins*:

- The Calvinistas[1] will attack Rob as a universalist.
- Rob won't care.
- *Christianity Today* will write a review that expresses some serious doubt and hesitation about Rob's new book, but they won't entirely throw him under the bus (yet).
- Rob won't care.
- Lots of people, like me, will blog about this.
- Rob won't care.
- Some people will even leave Mars Hill church because they don't like what's in the book.
- Rob won't care.

And, Bell, as if following these predictions as some kind of script, did exactly what Jones prophesied. He didn't care. He didn't respond to either the criticisms or the adulation. Bell didn't exploit or try to manage the debacle over whether or not he was a universalist. He simply moved on and began a speaking tour in fall 2011, "Fit to Smash Ice," which had nothing to do with *Love Wins* or with the controversy. Ruminating on Bell's *laissez-faire* attitude, Jones quipped, "It's a special gift to be able to be a theological provocateur

---

1 *Calvinista* is a kind of code term to identify contemporaries who police the Calvinist heritage, insuring that the sovereignty of God is maintained; the primacy of God's decision for us is always first.

and to be so un-codependent that you can say whatever you like with no fear. It seems to me that Rob Bell has that gift."[2]

This chapter maps out "that gift" as well as a variety of Bell's formative experiences that led to the development of his more subversive side. These events provide the necessary tools and benchmarks to understand Bell's critical eye when it comes to conventional wisdom and his unflagging ability to live above—or perhaps more accurately, below—the usual gossip and controversy over status and structure that dominate most establishment thinking.

From the beginning of his popularity, Bell has refused one type of Christian label after another: emergent, liberal, conservative, mainline, evangelical, neo-reformed, or Calvinist. Bell has disavowed them all. And so, when representatives from one or more of these Christian camps either take shots at or try to recruit Bell, as Jones explains, Bell refuses to "take the bait." He's not a "joiner." Bell moves in a world marked by what Victor Turner calls "liminality."[3]

This may be a strange term, but it's dead on. The term "liminality" describes a place in the world in which one is in the midst of transition, equality, simplicity, foolishness, and acceptance of pain—as opposed to the more conventional world in which stasis, hierarchy, shrewdness, prudence and avoidance of pain are what people seek and want. As a liminal figure, Bell lives "betwixt and between,"[4] and appears more than comfortable in that role.

He is unwilling to stop questioning. He refuses to say "this and only this is true," and he excavates buried questions, even when it makes everyone uncomfortable. In joining the ranks of liminal public figures, Bell unites the court jester, the prophet, and the Socratic

---

2 See Tony Jones' blog, "What's Up with Rob Bell?" February 28, 2011. http://www.patheos.com/blogs/tonyjones/2011/02/28/whats-up-with-rob-bell/. Accessed December 15, 2011.

3 "Liminal entities are neither here nor there; they are betwixt and between the positions assigned and arrayed by law, custom, convention, and ceremonial." In Victor Turner's "Liminality and Communitas," in *The Ritual Process: Structure and Anti-Structure.* Ithaca, NY: Cornell University Press, 1969, p. 94.

4 See Victor Turner, "Liminality and Communitas," pp. 106-7.

figure to poke, prod, and provoke conventional thinking. This is precisely what makes him so difficult to interpret and exactly why he is such a beguiling figure to try to explain.

The Early Days

Bell grew up in an all-American, upper-middle-class, Midwestern environment. It's not the kind of household one would expect to produce a subversive individual—especially one who would question some of the central canons of the conservative evangelical church in America, including how to approach the Bible, the very meaning of salvation, what worship should be and do, and the importance of certainty. Bell has retained an unremitting interest in asking questions; he entertains and even celebrates doubts. Even more controversially, as we will see in later chapters, Bell has been willing to challenge the ideology of American supremacy in the globe—an idea that is vital to many evangelicals and political conservatives in the United States. And all of this subversion grew in Bell despite his having been raised in a family that projected a conventional and conservative religious and political outlook.[5]

Bell grew up with a father who was a judge for Ingham County, East Lansing—Robert Holmes Bell. Next to Michigan's capital and near Michigan State University, this is a region less dominated by the Reformed Faith that is so typical of Western Michigan, where he would found Mars Hill. Bell's mother, a dynamic woman who had earned her master's degree from UCLA at 21, was a stay-at-home-mom who cared for her three children of whom Bell is the oldest.

Both parents had high standards, intellectually and religiously. Bell, a product of public schools, attended church twice a week at a Baptist congregation, but eventually the family moved to a

---

5 See Gregory Boyd's *The Myth of a Christian Nation: How the Quest for Political Power is Destroying the Christian Church.* Grand Rapids, MI: Zondervan, 2007. Boyd gave a very positive blurb for Bell's *Love Wins,* and Bell talked glowingly of Boyd's critique of the Christian Right. This book cost Boyd a third of church's membership.

nondenominational, evangelical church. Bell's father and mother strongly encouraged reading and asking questions; C.S. Lewis was "required reading." The family worked hard and played hard, but several events from those early years were telling and formative. Bell didn't personally experience the first event, but his father passed it to him as a legacy. Bell's grandfather died when his father was only eight, and family dynamics were such that one was not allowed to mourn the death of a Christian loved one. Bell's father was too young to understand why death and loss could not be mourned. Recalling his reaction to the death, Bell Sr. said, "We weren't allowed to mourn, because the funeral of a Christian is supposed to be a celebration of the believer in heaven with Jesus right now . . . But if you're eight years old, and your dad—the breadwinner—just died, it feels different . . .—sad."[6]

Rob Bell's reflections on the story mirror his deep-seated discomfort with being told how to feel or what to think. Bell understands the notion behind the directive not to cry, as demonstrated when he quipped: "To weep, to shed any tears—that would be doubting the sovereignty of God." This Calvinist dictum that God's ways are inscrutable and cannot be questioned stuck in Bell's craw, "That was the thing—they're all in heaven, so we're happy about that. It doesn't matter how you are actually humanly responding to this moment." And then in Rob Bell's patented ironic manner, he mused, "We're all just supposed to be thrilled." [7]

Early on, Bell learned from his parents that faith and critical thinking are important; dealing with emotions, however, can be not only complicated but also dangerous and needing negotiation. The success of his parents hid a good deal of ambivalence about their past and created an emotional legacy that Bell had to work through to establish his faith, sense of identity, and emotional well-being.

---

6 Jon Meachem, "Rob Bell: What If Hell Doesn't Exist?" *Time Magazine U.S.*, April 14, 2011. http://www.time.com/time/magazine/article/0,9171,2065289,00.html. Accessed July 9, 2012.

7 See Jon Meachem, "Rob Bell: What If Hell Doesn't Exist?"

The Reformed culture of Michigan, though more muted in East Lansing, was still potent in Bell's household. And though his father questioned the more dogmatic and sober theological heritage of the Reformed culture, Bell questioned it even more aggressively.

At an early age, Bell exhibited an emotional sensitivity to others—at least according to his parents. Rob Sr. recounted Bell's composure and awareness when they would visit sick friends and church members: "When he was around 10 years old, I detected that he had a great interest and concern for people. There he'd be, riding along with me, with his little blond hair, going to see sick folks or friends who were having problems, and he would get back in the truck after a visit and begin to analyze them and their situations very acutely. He had a feel for people and how they felt from very early on."[8]

This ability to traffic in people's emotions marked the family. It was less an emotional introspection than it was a way to understand, care for, and persuade others. His father was not only an excellent judge, but also politician with a deft touch. Bell's dad used his prodigious memory, a trait Bell inherited from him, to recall details from people's lives, oftentimes with precision that flabbergasted those around him. For instance, Bell could easily recall the names of people, the make of a car, or the memory that a door that was off a hinge, even twenty years after the fact.

Bell's father also impressed upon Bell the idea that the best witness to faith was not to speak about it explicitly, but to do one's job with excellence and professionalism. In the Bell family, professional success was a way to witness to the faith—a powerful source of Bell's passionate drive to succeed. For Bell, one demonstration of this lesson involves the sort of scriptural allusion that he himself is so fond of: "One of his [Rob Sr's] favorite things—he would talk about Daniel being the best possible advisor in the king's court and he would say, 'The bench is not a bully pulpit.' The way that you witness in

---

8 See Jon Meachem, "Rob Bell: What If Hell Doesn't Exist?"

the world is you do what you do to the very best of your ability with integrity and honesty and excellence."[9]

So, the ministry makeup bloomed in Bell's upbringing from early on. Bell's subversive side, however, ripened as well in his experience outside the comfortable confines of a relatively conventional and conservative Republican home life. In 1987, Ronald Reagan nominated Bell's father to the federal judiciary. He accepted; the senate confirmed him. And he still retains the position today. Bell's parents continue to be strong political conservatives.

This father who adores his son remains a towering figure and formative presence over Bell's history. Perhaps unsurprisingly, even as Bell lived into this deeply conservative Christian culture, he wrestled with its conventions and began to plot ways to transform it, even as he succeeded within it.

Early on, these traditional systems, whether religious or social, loomed over Bell as barriers rather than bridges. He explained, "In my school there were the Christian kids in the corner of the lunchroom with their sack lunches doing a Bible study or something, and then there were the athletes and cool kids. And I didn't really fit in with either. I had friends, but I grew up with a sense of—like . . . I just don't really fit in. I always felt like I didn't fit in."[10] For a person emotionally piqued by life's experience, the marginalization cut deep.

More to the point, the system's rules baffled him: "There were the kids for whom the system worked; they shined. I think of the kid with the locker next to me; he was every teacher's pet. He was the star athlete. It was just effortless for him. He seemed to have some sort of secret guidebook I didn't have."[11]

This is true for many young people growing up, but the depth of its effect on Bell is critical. In nearly every prayer and sermon of Bell's I listened to while writing this book, he speaks of the broken

---

9 Interview with Rob Bell by author, November 17, 2011.
10 Interview with Rob Bell by author, November 17, 2011.
11 Interview with Rob Bell by author, November 17, 2011.

hearted, the ones left behind, and those who have given up hope. Bell's deep empathy for the marginalized pulses through him as if he were speaking directly out of his own experience of exclusion, one that he knows in his bones, but also explored through his ministry. In Bell's first pastoral experience at Calvary Church in Grand Rapids, as an assistant to Ed Dobson, he made a point of seeking out and ministering to the most marginal: "I asked the front desk at Calvary Church, every single crisis call, every crazy person that throws a fit in the lobby, anyone who you suspect might be violent or suicidal, send them to me."[12] He relished the action and stimulation of working with people on the margins, trying to save them, and in turn, we might say, saving himself—for if they could find a place in the church, maybe he too had hope.

Ironically, in my second visit to Mars Hill on one of Bell's final Sundays, what was striking was the relative youth of the crowd, the shining spirit, middle class values, and Nordic appearance: hardly a group of the marginalized. Bell's consistent identification with the broken and lonely made me wonder what that crowd, then, actually represented. In a separate study of American megachurches, my colleagues and I analyzed a representative sample of twelve national megachurches and their members. Through more than 400 interviews with megachurch members, a robust set of needs, hidden wounds, and desires veritably flowed from nearly every person interviewed. Demographically, Mars Hill differs little from these other megachurches.

But just as important as Bell's empathy for those who do not "fit in" is his consistent experience of Jesus. This "Jesus mysticism," as he named it, gave him the tools to negotiate a childhood in which the emotional pain of exclusion cut deep. He described his rather conventional conversion experience of kneeling beside his bed to accept Jesus as his savior. The simplicity of this act, however, contrasted with the complexity of what Jesus came to mean to him. For Bell, the Jesus he imagined was the Jesus who subverted the dominant

---

12 Interview with Rob Bell by author, November 17, 2011.

system. Bell was consistently drawn to kids in the back row of the class: "There was something within me that was drawn to those for whom the system doesn't work like it's supposed to. That was deep in my bones. Jesus is for all of us who don't fit in."[13]

And so from these early feelings of alienation, Bell took on Jesus as his talisman, the marginal figure who scorned the system and befriended those outside it. Bell rejected organizations (whether school or church) that he saw doing nothing but "cranking out sausage," and kids "who followed the rules." Bell felt infused with an idea that he wanted to follow Jesus, the man who critiqued the system and drew to himself followers who were likewise on the margins.

In the midst of these moments of crisis and alienation, there were also flashes that he described as blissful and ecstatic. Bell recalled going to the U2 Joshua Tree Tour in 1987 at 16 years old. For most of the attenders, it was the "cool thing to do," but Bell wasn't concerned about fitting in. For him, it was purely about joy: "I remember thinking, nobody is talking about the experience as I experienced it . . . It was about a larger sense of intuitive connection, like a river that has always been flowing." This memory left an indelible mark on Bell's psyche, and the experience indicates a much broader concern in his own thought: "There is an eternal now that is present and available and near, and it has nothing to do with what most people are talking about."[14]

The quality of Bell's consciousness and his experience of this sense of timelessness and transcendence is a critical part of the rhetoric that pervades his life and ministry. This potent taste and sense of the divine in the midst of his life resonates in every part of his journey—a palpable feeling that God's spirit tracks his own.

Victor Turner, an anthropologist who studied African shamanic figures, aptly captures how Bell embodies a certain type of religious figure, "Prophets and artists tend to be liminal and marginal people, 'edgemen,' who strive with a passionate sincerity to rid themselves

---

13 Interview with Rob Bell by author, November 17, 2011.
14 Interview with Rob Bell by author, November 17, 2011.

of the clichés associated with status incumbency and role-playing and to enter into vital relationships with other men in fact or imagination."[15]

As an "edgeman," Bell follows the mystical feelings in his heart. Wrenched out of a system to which he can't relate, and in love with the man Jesus, whom he takes as his "edgeman," Bell stands against the system—whether it be the religious, political, or social system.

Edgeman is Educated

When one thinks of Wheaton College, the word *subversion* doesn't come to mind. The name *Billy Graham*, however, might. Other associations include teetotaler, and a puritanical and morally conservative form of Christianity. So when Bell entered Wheaton College in the fall of 1988, it is difficult to conceive of the decision as a move to subvert the system. Rather, it was a sure way to conform to it—in fact, to live into the groove of what many take as a relatively conventional conservative Christian college. After all it was only in 2003 that Wheaton College eased its ban on dancing and alcohol consumption *for faculty and staff.* However, it's important to consider that Wheaton has nurtured several scholars who have questioned some of the most pivotal conventions of the Christian Right.[16] Even within what appear to be established institutions, the Christian gospel has within it seeds of subversion, and Bell consumed these sources.

At Wheaton, Bell conquered his loneliness, and the story of his meeting his future wife sounds more like an evangelical fairy tale than the ruminations of a future subversive. Bell fondly recalls that

---

15 See Victor Turner's "Liminality and Communitas," p. 128.

16 See Mark Noll's *The Search for Christian America*, expanded edition. Colorado Springs, CO: Helmers & Howard Publishers, 1989. This book shows, rather conclusively, that America's founders never intended the nation to be Christian per se. See also Robert Webber's *Ancient-Future Faith: Rethinking Evangelicalism for a Postmodern World,* Grand Rapids, MI: Baker Academic, 1999. Webber has long been an important thinker for the emergent church movement.

in his first year at Wheaton, he met his wife, Kristen. The oft-repeated story is that, when they first met, he told her he was going to become a pastor, but when reminiscing over the event, Bell is fond of saying something to the effect of: "I don't think that was true; it was probably more a pick up line." Only at a school like Wheaton College would, "I want to be a pastor," be a pick up line. Though this seems an utterly conventional move, sometimes subversives use social structures to nurture their unique gifts, but it may simply be that Bell's future forms of subversion from within the Christian gospel were still dormant.

The irony was that in the midst of this "system" Bell fit in like a suffocating man who has just been given oxygen. From the context of a family and an early schooling where Bell felt a deep sense of alienation, at Wheaton College he experienced an explosion of creativity and surrounded himself with fellow "edgemen" taking his artistic bent to a kind of conversion-like threshold. College became Bell's laboratory for his performance art—studying ways not only to express himself but also to draw a crowd. The irony is that at this conventional choice of Wheaton—at least on the surface—the "edgeman" found more nurture and support than ever.

Bell describes it this way, "My particular little Wheaton world was unbelievably vibrant. My roommate and his friends had an improvisational comedy group called Seafood Rodeo. It was really alive, people making lots of really compelling and interesting stuff. So I was in a band, and friends were in indie bands. And all these different bands were getting together."[17]

Bell's own band life was intense and unintentionally short lived. His band "_ton bundle" played throughout his college career and actually landed gigs at several prominent venues in Chicago, leading Bell and the band to consider pursuing their music full-time. Early on, he roomed with Ian Eskelin who later formed the indie rock and Grammy nominated Christian band All Star United. These

---

17 Interview with Rob Bell by author, November 17, 2011.

were serious musicians. Listening to _ton bundle's *taking my donkey to town*, one picks up the tightness of the band and the quality of its sound.[18]

The band's audible references covered a range of styles in the 1990s—most prominently the list included the Talking Heads, Pixies, Violent Femmes, and Midnight Oil. The vocal lines and general style included early hip-hop and pop-funk rock, employing legato alternative-rock-style vocal lines and rap-like rhythmic speech. Bell, the group's primary lyricist and singer, sang songs that were conventional and full of romance and a young man's naiveté. Other songs evoked faith and God in poetic and esoteric terms. On one such track, called "inbetweens and afterwards," the chorus pleads, "Fill this soul with something sweet/Fill this spirit with something you need."

The songs also share Bell's goofiness. For example, in the song "And I. Am. Happy.," the chorus includes the nonsensical statement, "Fuzzy Wuzzy was a bear, and donkeys have a kind of off color grey hair." Another song is an early rendition of "velvet elvis," a reference in anticipation of Bell's first book by the same title. The song lyrics were sonically blurred and involved using a faux, deep south, African-American dialect that was racialized and strange. Needless to say, the sound of the band trumped its lyrics in quality, though the writing, in its poetic and staccato verse, anticipated the style of Bell's later writings.

All of this ended in fall 1991. Bell was in his senior year of college, and the band was readying for their first major tour, starting in Chicago. But a strange headache hit Bell, and, as he explained, "I took some aspirin, laid on the couch, and waited for it to go away. But it didn't; it got worse. By midnight I was in agony, and by 3 a.m., I was wondering if I was going to die. As the sun rose, my roommate drove me to the hospital where I learned that I had viral

---

18 Rob Bell, *taking my donkey to town: Greatest Hits 1989-1992*, with Brian Erickson; Chris Fall, and David Houk,1992 by battle cabbage music. Compact disc.

meningitis."[19] The musical dream died. With the tour cancelled, the band went their separate ways. Bell explained to me, "It was sad, and it was inevitable."

All Bell's work, patience, and "restless energy" had been put in the direction of a music career. But Bell's energy had been cut off just as he was beginning to rise: "As this reality hit me, laying there in that hospital bed miles from home with a brain infection, I distinctly remember asking no one in particular 'Now what?' "[20]

Wheaton gave Bell a place to let his creative energies expand, allowing them to be exposed to all sorts of artistic outlets. It's no surprise that music was his art of choice—a marginal, creative, energetic outlet for a lead man, with a voice, ready and wanting to go public. During the music period of his life at Wheaton, Bell pushed school and academics to the side. Wheaton provided structure in which performers could be studied, and a platform for Bell to find other artists with whom to collaborate. Performing pumped his blood, so the choice between studying or going to hear a band or speaker was never a choice—the latter *always* won out.

And this energy to be on the stage motivated him. Strangely, what stimulated Bell's turn to the dream of ministry was, in fact, a rather conventional event. He went to a lecture delivered by C. Everett Koop, the former Surgeon General under Ronald Reagan. "I went to hear him give a lecture for some odd reason, and I was sitting waiting for the lecture to start, and nobody had taken their seats around me, and I was sitting there and having this moment, 'I should go to seminary.' And literally like a full body sort of moment, that's what I'm going to do. Alright, I'll do that."[21]

Bell communicated this transformation in multiple frames. The experience at the Koop event may have been critical, but his work at Honey Rock, a Wheaton-sponsored Christian camp for young people, was determinative. There he preached when no one else could, "I

---

19 See Jon Meachem's "Rob Bell: What If Hell Doesn't Exist?"
20 See Jon Meachem's "Rob Bell: What If Hell Doesn't Exist?"
21 Interview with Rob Bell by author, November 17, 2011.

didn't know anything. I took off my Birkenstocks beforehand. I had this awareness that my life would never be the same again."[22]

In his book, *Velvet Elvis*, Bell explains it as a "voice" he hears, though "not audible," nonetheless, telling him, "teach this book, and I will take care of everything else."[23] The meningitis rocked Bell's life course, and the act of preaching channeled his enormous energies. "Now I had something I could do with my life. In that moment by the side of the lake, barefoot, with my tongue-tied and my heart on fire; I found something I could give my life to."[24]

There is nothing particularly subversive in the move to preaching, and the decision to go to seminary from Wheaton College could not have been more conventional. However, from the perspective of a conservative evangelical culture, the choice of seminaries was. Fuller Theological Seminary in California—a moderate, evangelical, nondenominational seminary—had more than 4,000 students from 70 countries and more than 100 denominations. It created a space so diverse and free of coercion that Bell's boundaries sometimes forcibly expanded even further.

At Fuller, Bell honed his ability to communicate. If nothing else, the public side of Bell begged to perform. Revealingly, at the Times 100 gala—honoring *Time Magazine*'s 100 Most Influential People, Bell told the story of Bill Pannell, the legendary African-American preacher who mentored Bell at Fuller. After listening to a young student's dreadful sermon delivery, Pannell walked up and began to read the manuscript with a tone and intonation that transformed the words. Bell was mesmerized. "It's how you're reading, it isn't just what you're saying, it's how you're saying it. Soul can do all kinds of things, if you have it."[25] Bell wouldn't forget this lesson; one might have the content, but without a voice that attracts, nothing happens.

---

22 See Meachem's "Rob Bell: What If Hell Doesn't Exist?"
23 Rob Bell, *Velvet Elvis: Repainting the Christian Faith,* Grand Rapids, MI: Zondervan, 2005, p. 40.
24 Rob Bell, *Velvet Elvis*, p. 41.
25 Interview with Rob Bell by author, November 17, 2011.

Bell's subversive side flourished in the Fuller system. He realized that despite all the denominational differences, the boundaries not only don't count, but they also miss the point. Jesus liberated his followers to transform and free his people. As Bell explained, "Fuller took my intuition of a boundary-less journey . . . and amped it up." When he realized that loyalty to any one denomination did not matter to him, he felt free. But in this freedom, Bell sought a mentor. And he found one in Ed Dobson. In 1995, Bell went with his new wife, Kristen, and his fire to speak to study under Dobson at Calvary Church in Grand Rapids.

Dobson, in his own way, subverted conventions. An early supporter and leader for Jerry Falwell's Moral Majority, in 1987 Dobson left his position at Falwell's Liberty University and became the pastor of Calvary Church. Moody Bible Institute recognized him as a *pastor extraordinaire* in 1993, and in 2001, when he was diagnosed with Lou Gehrig's disease, Dobson struggled but continued in ministry and writing, penning *The Year of Living Like Jesus* in 2009. That same year, he cemented his "subversion" of the Christian Right by claiming on *Good Morning America* that he had voted for Barack Obama in the 2008 presidential election. Why? Because he thought that Obama was "closer to Jesus's teachings."[26]

Dobson welcomed Bell's 1998 decision to start a church. Bell reported that "around 300 Calvary Church congregants" came along with him on his adventure—to start a church that would prove to be subversive—a church that would be, in Bell's words, "like a rock

---

26 Dobson's comments caused great controversy, particularly because of the implications on conservative Christians' stance on abortion as well as Dobson's position at Cornerstone University in Grand Rapids; Dobson responded, "For me, being pro-life includes not only the protection of the unborn but also how we treat people who are already born. I felt that Mr. Obama was closer to the essence of Jesus' teachings—compassion for the poor and the oppressed, being a peacemaker, loving your enemies and other issues. I have also said, though it never was printed, that I have little faith in politicians of either party." http://www.mlive.com/living/grand-rapids/index.ssf/2009/01/cornerstone_president_ed_dobso.html. Accessed February 4, 2012.

show, in the sense that people would like be to there."[27] Two and a half years later, 10,000 people were coming to Bell's rock shows—Mars Hill church landed on the map.

Kill the Superpastor

What happens to a person when everything works on their first attempt? Bell's success tested that question. Attracting 10,000 people nearly overnight dropped a bomb into the evangelical world. Preaching Sunday after Sunday on the book of Leviticus could not have been a more dissonant way to build a career, but that's what Bell did. He stripped down the service to bare bones, using an indie band, employing the whole congregation as the "choir" and "amping" up his messages with various props and gimmicks: lighting objects on fire, filling the stage with plants, and even bringing in live animals. The "ritual master" wanted to be noticed. And he was.

But the edgeman tilted. Bell lamented the "dark side" of his success. [28] In the middle of his triumph, he began to question the very foundations of many evangelical conventions—important ones. He insisted that a "personal relationship with Jesus Christ," or "inviting Jesus into your heart," had no foundation in scripture. Moreover, Bell thought the very notion of "eternal salvation" signaled an "evacuation" of the earth to heaven, arguing that this idea was extrabiblical. For Bell the core biblical message centered on the principle that, "Salvation is the entire universe being brought back into harmony with its maker."[29]

Not only did evangelical conventions drop like boulders off the cliffs of Bell's consciousness, something even more fundamental rocked his internal world. Channeling his own darkness, Bell explained, "No amount of success can heal a person's soul."[30] And Bell's demons had a source: "Things happened to me when I was thirteen

---

27 Interview with Rob Bell by author, November 17, 2011.
28 Rob Bell, *Velvet Elvis*, p. 103.
29 Rob Bell, *Velvet Elvis*, p. 109.
30 Rob Bell, *Velvet Elvis*, p. 110.

that have shaped me."[31] Bell recalled an incident that consisted of his rejection by the popular group at school—hardly catastrophic. But combined with Bell's teen angst and a complicated family life that shined on the surface but hid deeper layers of dysfunction, Bell struggled with marginalization in school, wrestling to understand it all. That journey of self-discovery and his struggle to integrate it nurtured his empathy and insight into the human condition. In part, the drive to succeed in the Bell family turned on him—and also marked his siblings, as we will discover.

Because of Bell's talent and drive, his success flourished beyond anyone's dreams. In fact, Bell recalled that many warned him not to expect "more than a 100 people in the church in the first year." His success was built on employing unusual strategies. The idea of advertising the church, for example, made him sick: "This is not a product, this not an enterprise for which you put a billboard out."[32] Rather, he wanted word of the church to spread through human contact, with members bringing in a constant stream of new people through word of mouth. Bell refused and rejected signs that marked the church's location. The church's success would be on his terms.

Nevertheless, the empty space, the darkness inside of him could not be filled. Even in the midst of enormous numbers coming to his church and people from across the country wanting to meet him and hear him speak, Bell was not able to silence the questions in his heart or find the peace he desired. Not finding solace in church, he turned to counseling and to his wife, Kristen, for guidance.

This turn away from the spotlight and the adulation of the crowd would profoundly shape how Bell changed during his tenure at Mars Hill. As he said about himself, "I'm an epic people pleaser."[33] But he learned that his "true" identity was not in pleasing everyone but in *making things*. Bell dropped out. He couldn't sit in the church office. He couldn't stomach the long church meetings, and in many ways,

---

31 Rob Bell, *Velvet Elvis*, p. 112.
32 Interview with Rob Bell by author, November 17, 2011.
33 Interview with Rob Bell by author, May 29, 2012.

he paid dearly for this subversion. Ultimately, the cost of his success was the person that he wanted to be. The delivery of a rock star performance and the demands produced by his followers damaged his faith, so Bell made a hard decision. In *Velvet Elvis*, Bell reflected on that crisis and explained his choice: "I had to kill superpastor."[34]

Bell wanted to build a movement, not a church. As he explained, "Let's move buildings every couple of years, just to make sure no one gets attached." Nonetheless, Mars Hill quickly outgrew their Wyoming school gym, and they bought the Grand Village Mall for $1 in their first year, moving into the remodeled anchor store in July 2000 but Bell still refused to see Mars Hill as an institution, viewing it as a "gathering of people." Or, as he put in his last letter to his church in 2011, continuing his habit of using lowercase letters and haphazard punctuation:

> who ARE mars hill.
> so when people say what's going to happen to mars hill?
> they're asking what's going to happen to you. what are you going to do. how are you going to respond?
> you are the answer,
> because you are the church.
> mars hill is not a product,
> it is a gathering of people.
> you.
> that's why there's no sign.
> how does a person find mars hill?[35]

Of course, maintaining this "flesh and blood, breathing, living people," over the twelve years of his tenure challenged every side of Bell. In those early years, as Mars Hill grew, Bell pushed further away from the initial connection with Calvary Church. Bell kept close to

---

34 Rob Bell, *Velvet Elvis*, p. 115.

35 Sermon, "Rob Bell's Parting Epistle to Mars Hill: "Grace + Peace," December 19, 2011. In *Sojourners: Faith in Action for Social Justice*, Cathleen Falsani. http://sojo.net/blogs/2011/12/19/rob-bells-parting-epistle-mars-hill-grace-peace. Accessed January 5, 2012.

Dobson, but he rejected many of Calvary's restrictions on women in leadership as well as its formality, liturgy, and church bureaucracy. Bell's early initiative to allow women as elders at Mars Hill had push back—more than 1,000 parishioners left Mars Hill in protest. For Bell equality demanded this leveling, and Bell's own internal compass contested the conventional gender and power hierarchies in the typical megachurch model. Bell took no degrees or titles and, perhaps more pointedly, built no more buildings. Under Bell, Mars Hill gave away more than a quarter of what they took in through their "joy boxes," twice as high as the average megachurch in the nation.[36] Bell distanced himself and his church not only from Calvary but from most evangelical churches—Bell, ever the edgeman, was carving his own path in a notoriously conformist church culture.

Bell maintained the liminal nature of his calling, refusing the conventional status markers and eschewing the theological clichés in his evangelical circles. He also embraced the pain and suffering in his own life as well as in the lives of those in his congregation. As he reflected in *Velvet Elvis*, "I cannot lead people somewhere I am not trying to go myself . . . and that's why for so many the church experience has been so shallow—so many leaders have never descended into the depths of their own souls."[37] Bell began to mine the gold from his own depths, using his own suffering, the places betwixt and between in him, to share, heal, and give solace to his church.

Subversive Suffering

Subversive suffering is the kind that frees the soul to live in the liminal state and to be at peace in the midst of the betwixt and between. Bell's willingness to go into these depths marked his ministry with a focus on allowing tensions to stand. He made a choice to look at

---

36 Statistics are in my article with Katie Corcoran and Kate Stockly-Meyerdirk. "'God is like a Drug': Interaction Ritual Chains in American Megachurches." *Journal for the Social Scientific Study of Religion*, (under review); for further reading, see my forthcoming book *High on God*.

37 Rob Bell, *Velvet Elvis*, p. 119.

the depths of suffering and lean into them while learning from them and to innovate in his thinking and feeling as old constructs revealed themselves as useless.

The pain that Bell faced in his own life surfaced in his brother's life as well. In a 2008 sermon about the letter to the Philippians, Bell struck a somber note in his sermon by describing the context of the letter, with Paul's imprisonment in a Roman jail, before meditating on Paul's words, "Grace and peace to you from God our Father and the Lord Jesus Christ." And Bell then repeated the phrase more than fifty times over the course of the sermon: "Have it at the front of your heart, grace and peace to you; grace and peace on your past; grace and peace on your present; grace and peace between us; grace and peace in all things."[38] And he ended the sermon by calling up his brother.

As John Bell arrived on the stage, he told the simple but dramatic story of his personal recovery and restoration from drug and alcohol addiction. Not unlike his older brother, the story was a series of short glimpses into a troubled life, not sparing himself at all, "The reason I'm sharing my story . . . it's not because I'm his brother but because of the grace and peace that has been extended to me over the last four years."

In his story, John Bell described a young boy who on the surface pleased everyone, a family who believed in him, and a young man who didn't believe in himself: "The problem was from middle school through college, why would these people love me so much when I clearly didn't deserve it and certainly screw up what they wanted for me." He described a series of addictions to drugs, alcohol, and pornography and an eventual life of drug dealing in college. That road ended in failure and desolation, including the loss of connections with family, friends, and his then girlfriend. John explained that he was depressed and emotionless, and would sometimes cry for long periods of time:

---

38 Rob Bell, "Grace and Peace," Mars Hill Bible Church, Grandville, MI, January 6, 2008. Sermon. MP3.

The shame I felt for the person I had become was unbe-
lievable. I couldn't remember a time when I had believed in
God, and I didn't have a working relationship with anyone in
my family. The people who had been closest to me I pushed
out of my life, I felt very alone. After one particularly hard
weekend, my brother called me on Tuesday, November 11.
He and my sister and parents could not take it any longer,
and what he said to me that afternoon was the beginning of
the biggest and best change of my life. He said to me, "You
are living in hell right now." And all I could say, was "Yes, I
am." He said, "What would you do to change that?"

Rob Bell then led his younger brother through an intervention, and
John described the long, hard road of recovery as beginning in this
manner: "The day after my first meeting, I attended Mars Hill, I
came to the 11:00 service and sat right over there, and I couldn't stop
crying, people I hardly knew were giving me hugs, telling me I was
going to be okay. For the first time, I felt that something was happening to me. The thing was happening to me, I'm now convinced
was that I was being saved."

The end was John Bell's recovery and reunion with family and
friends and faith. Rob Bell then returned to the stage and ended the
sermon with a plea: "Mars Hill finds it unacceptable for those in our
midst . . . to struggle alone." He invited those in need to come forward
and to be ministered to by counseling professionals around the stage.

Bell's bookended comments on grace and peace remained somber. This was no triumph but an exploration of his brother's wounds
and a meditation about the grace and peace that had transformed his
own life.

In 2008, Bell moved into the deeper waters of his own wounds.
For the coming summer, he asked his elders for space and time to
think: "I had this overwhelming sense that I was to stop speaking
publically for awhile; it was like this deep sense of God going 'sit
down and be quiet.'" He went to Ireland, and he walked alone along
the sea, finding solace and wise words in an Irish priest. There, he

heard a new word, "Rob, you have been told a lie . . . that you have all this control and power. You don't. All that is left for you to do is to give yourself to your work. Give yourself away and enjoy it."[39]

The full fruit of Bell's understanding of subversive suffering came that following year in his 2009 sermon series, and his exegesis of the Sermon on the Mount. Reading the text "Blessed are the poor in spirit, for theirs is the kingdom of heaven," (Matt 5:3) Bell suggested that being poor in spirit was not a goal or prescription, not something to be "obtained," nor a "praise worthy condition." Jesus' announcement was this: "God is on the side of everybody when there is no reason to be on their side." Bell then laid out the implications of this radical claim, "Blessed are all the wretched people, the losers, blessed are the ones who don't believe in God. Blessed are all the people who have no reason to be blessed." [40]

Rhetorically, Bell came back to the question of why God would bless the ones who have not been worthy of their blessing. Why does God do this? Because, Bell explained, "God is like this." He then laid out the implications of the text and his interpretation, looking at the congregation in front of him and announcing, "All the people in this section who have had an abortion, God is on your side. All the people who have been unfaithful to their spouse, God loves you. To those who go to all the wrong websites, the kingdom of heaven is available to you."

Subversive suffering, for Bell, is discovering the full implications of a God who dwells in the liminal nature of human life and blesses these in-between places that the conventionally "religious" scoff at and condemn. Bell follows the subversive figure of Jesus, who blesses the "zeroes" and the "outsiders." For Bell this claim is the keystone of the gospel he proclaims: "For those who have done all the wrong things, and who may not even believe in grace, this grace is there for them."

---

39 Rob Bell, ": Ecclesiastes Part 1: Lessons in Vapor Management," Mars Hill Bible Church, Grandville, MI, January 9, 2011. Sermon. MP3.

40 Rob Bell, "Poor in Spirit," Mars Hill Bible Church, Grandville, MI, September 13, 2009. Sermon. MP3.

This insight subverts the taken-for-granted distance between what is sacred and what is profane. How to interpret what is religious and what is not. How to negotiate systems of power and powerlessness. How individuals manage the avoidance of pain and confusion and what is the embracing of pain, suffering, and confusion. The liminal nature of Bell's own condition parallels and recapitulates the gospel Bell finds in Jesus.

Jesus is Bell's edgeman, the liminal figure who stands not to embody a status system of the religious, or a system of control, or a system that avoids suffering but who stands to call followers back into places where the conventional avenues of status and success don't count. In these spaces, control no longer matters, pain is faced and suffering and loss are blessed, and the betwixt and between of life are in fact the very place that the sacred dwells. This dark green line flows through Bell at the end of his ministry at Mars Hill. It puts the lie to those calling him to stop the questioning, embody his status, control his people, and affirm a theological "norm." He simply says no.

"Well, that's easy for someone who is charismatic, talented, and rich," critics say. And all of that may be true. For some, it comes down to the question of hypocrisy. Is Bell a charismatic hypocrite? Can anyone who succeeds truly continue to embody this subversive message? The question hovers and haunts this book, not only for Bell but for anyone who claims to follow a Lord who calls people "to take up their cross daily and follow" (Luke 9:23, CEB).

chapter three

CHARISMA

Got no salvation
Got no religion
Tell me something that'll save me
I need a man who makes me alright
My religion is you

Lady Gaga, "Teeth," The Fame Monster, *2009*

Lady Gaga, the queen of pop, made a splash with *The Fame Monster* EP, harking back to 1980's Glam Rock, skewering fashion show runways. She demonstrated the charisma of mega-celebrities strutting their stuff, and, without stretching too much, piercing the "charismatic bond" that is so potent to the megachurch pastor success over the last several decades, and certainly for Rob Bell.

Many who read this book will suspect that Bell isn't what he's cracked up to be or recognize him as an enigmatic religious figure. This work aims to penetrate these puzzles. Lady Gaga gets right what many distrust about pastoral leaders who perfectly mirror the feelings and thoughts of their hearers and then channel what their hearers want to find in themselves: "My religion is you." Hers is an attack on figures that play proxy to the hopes and dreams of a generation searching for the answer to their problems—a way to pierce through the persona of those who pledge to lead people to the promised land. These figures become objects of reverence, as well as points of envy or even loathing. Bell provokes these same feelings on all sides and effortlessly exemplifies the charismatic bond that is central to this story.

Bell certainly has "the gift." In *Rain,* his inaugural 12-minute film of the twenty-four set *Nooma* collection, Bell's classic collection of traits is on display. The setting is a Bell family vacation in the deep woods. Bell starts on an early walk with his one year-old son, Trace. The scene is one of bucolic bliss with an edgy, moody guitar playing in the background—set against a cloudless sky. Bell opens with a wondering statement: "Do you ever have those moments? If you could just freeze them . . . just so beautiful." And instantly the observer tumbles into this timeless moment of a dad and his son on an early morning walk. As they round the lake there is a twist in the story, clouds move in, and Bell narrates, "It starts to rain. It always rains, doesn't it?"

On cue, Bell tells the biblical story of Jesus and his kingdom. He recounts the parable of the wise and foolish builders—one who builds his life on sand and another on rock (Matt 7:24-27). When the rains and the storms come, the first is destroyed and the second stands. The person who has built his life on sand has "rejected Jesus' teachings," but the one who built his life on the rock, and has "come to follow Jesus," will withstand any storms that come—that will always come.

In the film, the rain comes slowly at first, and then begins to pour. Bell takes his son Trace off his back and puts him close to his chest, and as the rain envelops them, Trace wails at the top of his lungs. Bell bundles his son to his chest, and coos with deep passion, "I love you buddy, we're going to make it, dad knows the way home. We're going to make it." Immediately, Bell's narration smoothly moves to a discussion of the Psalms, where God's people cry out over and over again to God, and God promises that he will listen.

Bell explains, "There is this false and twisted idea in the church that God is looking for people who have no problems . . . The essence of salvation is admitting, 'I don't have it altogether.' Jesus says, 'I'm not looking for the healthy but the sick.'"

Like the father in the story of the prodigal son, Bell models here the relationship between God and humanity; God hears the cry of the vulnerable one: listening, comforting, and guiding the prodigal home. Bell ends the film with this benediction, "Now may you when you're soaking wet, when you're confused, may you cry out, and may the creator of the universe hold you tight and may you hear him say, 'I love you buddy, dad knows the way home, we're going to make it.'"

The film evokes wildly contrasting emotions of bliss, terror, intimacy, fear, being lost, and being found. It promises comfort even in the midst of terrible distress. All of this is combined with a message that in Christ, the lost and confused believer who builds her life on the rock is still held in God's hands, close to God's heart.

It's a remarkable debut of Bell's ability to engage the viewer, the listener, the follower on so many different levels. Artistically, it is noteworthy because the complexity of emotion is communicated in a short film. The visuals and the musical score, along with Bell's voice, tone, and intonation effortlessly arouse the feelings of the moment in which the viewer sees a transparent portrayal of what a good father will do in the midst of the reality of life's catastrophes.

The *Nooma* films all have a similarly simple and artistic feel, as if produced on a small budget, yet each cost $100,000 to $200,000, involved up to 40 people, and required at least twenty script rewrites. When given the script, Bell would memorize it quickly and often deliver the lines flawlessly the first time through.

Fatefully, the filming for *Rain* was done on 9/11. One of the producers recalled the experience of shooting on such a tumultuous day: "Filming started the morning of September 11, 2001. The towers were down, and we didn't know if there was going to be a government by nightfall because the Pentagon was on fire. We didn't know if we should keep going or not."[1] The charismatic bond builds on social crisis and a talented leader who can communicate the thoughts and feelings of followers and can offer, in word and in action, a way out. "It rains; it always rains."

The Charismatic Bond

We usually attribute charisma to the talent of one individual. And individual talent counts, but charisma is a sociological phenomenon.[2] Charismatic individuals arise most often during social crises—a major disruption to the cultural system that sends out echoes of alienation into the cultural bloodstream. And so, charisma in its essence is a relationship between a leader and their followers, with a leader providing a model and method for managing crises. At its heart, charisma is a "bond" that is about influence, both delicate and complex.

A close church friend and collaborator of Bell's described the bond this way: "He has what I call an 'it' factor . . . but it's like a gas gauge meter, and everybody has some "it" factor . . . Rob's is super high. He walks into a room, and the whole room is altered."[3] In countless interviews, this same "influence" surfaced with nearly everyone to whom I spoke about Bell; in fact, many spontaneously called him one of their "best friends."

Bell's ability to connect with others was an asset he built on from the beginning of his tenure at Mars Hill church. Nearly overnight, two to three months into starting the church, between 4,000 and 6,000 people were coming to services, and in the second year 10,000 were attending. Such numbers were drawn, at least partially, by the fact that the mutual regard between Bell and his following was contagious and potent.

---

1 Interview with Bell associate by author, November 19, 2011.

2 Max Weber, the German sociologist and political theorist, analyzed the sociological realities of charismatic figures, both religious and political. See Weber's *Economy and Society: An Outline of Interpretive Sociology.* NY, Bedminster Press, 1968.

3 Interview with Rob Bell associate by author, November 19, 2011.

From his early sermons at Mars Hill, the love and affection that he showered on the congregation was remarkable and consistent. At the beginning of one of the sermons, he stated (to a crowd of thousands), "Hello, my best friends!" The joy and the affection in his countenance were disarming, the response overwhelming from the crowd. Calling a group of 10,000 people "my best friends" strikes many as bizarre, but the enthusiasm of the response testified to the reciprocal nature of the affection from the audience—the charismatic bond in action.

As one of the leaders at Mars Hill explained, "He's more comfortable in a group of a hundred people or a thousand people than he is in a group of two if he doesn't know who you are. A thousand strangers is fine for him, but close up, it's a little tougher."[4] And yet despite speaking to such large crowds, people expressed sentiments during interviews similar to, "I feel like he is speaking just to me."

Bell's capacity for intimacy with his hearers is related to his ability to articulate the emotional dilemma of those listening and then speak to their concerns with a perspicuity that is jarring, but also with a boldness and certitude that flow from a kind of youthful naiveté. For example, a man who would become one of Bell's closest associate lay leaders described his experience of hearing one of Bell's early sermons. He had been invited to come to hear Bell; and reluctantly he did. Having grown up in the Christian Reformed tradition, this man had turned his back on it precisely because of its religious and moral dogmatism. And as he narrates, "I'd heard some things about him. So I went. I really wasn't paying attention. I just couldn't wait to leave. Rob gets up, and the teaching was God does not need you. I'm like, shit. I'm the center of my universe, how can He not need me? Isn't heaven collapsing, if there is one, without my leadership?"[5]

Bell's early preternatural surety was on full display. God doesn't need anyone. It was paradoxical intention, a device Bell returned to

---

4 Interview with Rob Bell associate by author, November 19, 2011.
5 Interview with Rob Bell associate by author, November 19, 2011.

in many of his later sermons. When listeners are told that they aren't needed, it ups the ante; they feel even more drawn in than before.

The same leader continues by quoting lines from Bell's same sermon, "'Because if God is not on the throne, you are. It's either one or the other. And it's a struggle.' So I walked out of there, going, what in the world was that? This wasn't like this fabulous 'Come to me, Jesus.' It was none of it. And that's when I understood for the first time that God is real, and the Holy Spirit is acting and moving. I don't care what anybody says, because I had an encounter."

Many affirmed, explained, or implied a similar experience. Bell stimulates thought often by association or striking metaphors, and sometimes with the use of antitheses, as we saw with *Rain,* in which comfort and suffering play off of each other. This rhetoric affects many and suggests change, even outright transformation. Through these strategies, Bell facilitates a powerful bond between himself and his audience.

Bell's rhetoric is a result of his own complex affective experience in faith. Bell discovered in his relationship with Jesus a nearly "ecstatic" experience as well as an immense amount of power and meaning. This experiential significance came out over and over again in our interviews and in his sermons. The emotional salience of his relationship with Jesus consistently acts as a catalyst for the transformation of others.

In another case, with a friend and fellow minister, Bell's experience of scripture literally saved the faith of his friend. Bell's friend explained it this way,

> We go to the back and we were waiting to set up for their first service Wednesday night, and we're sitting in the back of the auditorium, and Rob takes out his notepad and says, "This is stuff I'm learning." At this point, it's Hebrew stuff he is applying to understanding God and he's so excited about it. And it has nothing to do with what he is going to speak about that night. He is just voracious about learning at this point. And then he looks at me and says these words I will never ever forget. Rob said, "There's hardly a day that goes by that I

am not drawn to tears on what I'm discovering in scripture." Now for somebody who is in a crisis of faith, who believed there was nothing left to discover and was finding in ministry it wasn't working, people weren't responding anymore. It opened up a door for me. It took me three years to figure out what do I believe, and to wade through all this crap, and begin a journey of reconstructing. That kind of thing Rob Bell has done for thousands and thousands of people at their own levels.[6]

This is the charismatic bond: a person or group in crisis meeting someone who empathizes and communicates the feelings of that crisis and who can then respond, with deep empathy, about how they have gotten through. Bell, having taken his own journey into the darkness, acts as a proxy, or perhaps more pertinently as a midwife—enabling followers to birth what he often describes as the "non-anxious certitude of faith" in the midst of crisis that he communicates in books, sermons, film, and in person.

Charismatic Context

Context matters in the charismatic relationship, and the context for Bell's work at Mars Hill was critical to his success. Western Michigan is one of the cultural centers of the Reformed Church in America, and as any number of Bell's associates told me, Bell was a "breath of fresh air" in a cultural and religious hothouse of Dutch Calvinism— a theological brew that draws on a Calvinist code of theology and that follows a strict and restrictive set of traditional dogmatic and moral principles.

The nature of Calvinism, particularly within the American setting has had enormous impact on cultures ranging from American Puritanism to the Scotch Irish in the South and Southwest, the Presbyterians in the Middle Atlantic, including the Dutch Calvinists who moved into Michigan from their original setting in New

---

6 Interview with a Rob Bell associate, November 17, 2011.

York.[7] As one of Bell's associates explained, "The theology has an acronym, TULIP, which is fun for the Dutch people because of the flowers and the Dutch; it stands for total depravity, unconditional election, limited atonement, irresistible grace, and the perseverance of the saints—once saved always saved; but the whole thing about the teaching is that there are the elect and then there are the reprobate, and you either are or you aren't."[8] It's hard not to overestimate the power of this movement and its impact on American culture. The story is long and complicated, but for many, particularly in the region of Western Michigan, this culture has formed their thinking and believing about faith.

Contrary to what many assert, even the purest form of Calvinism never promised certitude about heaven. In fact in early Reformed theology, God predestines most of humanity to hell. Salvation is a gift to the few, but even those few are never sure of it. In this way, insecurity gripped many Calvinists who became rigidly obedient to Christian precepts in an attempt to assure their own salvation. This created in many a vigorous attitude toward work, so named "the Protestant work ethic," designed to illustrate in worldly terms success and a sense of God's blessing.[9] It is no wonder then that many sought out ways to mitigate the intensity of this theological tradition.

In fact, the most important twentieth century Reformed theologian, Karl Barth, speculated that in God's goodness, all may be predestined to salvation, since Christ "to reconciled all things to himself" (Col 1:20, CEB). So the movement away from double predestination (some destined for hell and some for heaven) and the

---

7 The most informative book on Calvinism and its deep impact on the thought, culture and politics of America is David Hackett Fischer's *Albion's Seed: The Four British Folkways in America*. Oxford University Press, 1989. And more specifically about the Dutch, Randall Balmer's *A Perfect Babel of Confusion: Dutch Religion and English Culture in the Middle Colonies*. NY: Oxford University Press, 2002.

8 Interview with Rob Bell associate by author, November 18, 2011.

9 See Max Weber's *The Protestant Ethic and the Spirit of Capitalism*. Translated by Talcott Parsons, NY: Charles Scribner's Sons, 1950.

debate over universalism (all are chosen for heaven) has been a part of the conversation in Reformed communities for at least a century. Nonetheless, the shadow of a demanding theological worldview lingers.

Bell's movement away from dogmatic obedience and fear-driven focus on doctrines of the faith to a more gracious and "non-anxious" attitude toward God caught many as not only attractive but also enormously welcome as they experienced Bell's philosophy of ministry. Nearly all the associates and friends whom I interviewed had similar tales of this sense of liberation, renewal, and regeneration of faith because of the kind and quality of the message Bell presents.

Bell's sermons and various teachings create a rich field of inquiry into the Christian faith that celebrates thought, questions, and doubts about the deepest aspects of faith and scripture. Bell displays to his listeners a bold and, what they would call, "courageous" exploration of faith and the Bible. Many of those who I interviewed reported that it is precisely this 'exploration' that set them free from past roadblocks and the fear that they felt percolating and penetrating their psyches as a result of the Reformed Church's theology. In this sense, for Bell, spiritual transformation clearly trumps belief; flesh-and-blood experience of God's love overcomes dogma and doctrine. And probing questions of scripture are more faithful than proclamations of inerrancy.

This is precisely what a charismatic principal does. He describes the dilemma, a system that depresses rather than releases thought and action, and then he offers plausible alternatives, ways of thinking of God as a source of energy that releases boundless forms of creative purpose in the world, announcing all the ways that a person might use these energies to express their human potential for growth, inquiry, and creativity. Most importantly, this leader acts as a proxy, showing effective ways that this message releases them with energy, love, and creative action in the world.

Hearers feel a deep sense of empathy and understanding for their particular dilemma, and a sure confidence that the solutions offered are reasonable and have worked for the person who communicates them. Herein lies a test for the charismatic leader. Can such a leader explain the problem and offer solutions as well as live those out in the world? This is the question we have of all charismatic leaders: Does the life match the performance? Is the charisma real and authentic? Or is it "just" an act?

Charisma and Hypocrisy

At the heart of hypocrisy is the art of playing a part, to play act. Every charismatic figure, in order to create and secure the charismatic bond, must play the part in such a way that people believe what they are saying is not only true but also real in their life. While Bell admits awareness of this dynamic, he uncannily deflects and ignores his detractors. For some, it remains a concern. Bell's unique ability to perform is something he clearly nurtures in his life and ministry.

On the last day of my visit to Mars Hill I attended the two services led by Bell. The first service was simple and direct, beginning with several songs and then moving to a teaching. The hymn preceding the teaching was an updated version of Isaac Watts' 1719 *Our God, Our Help in Ages Past*. Troy Hatfield, the leader of Mars Hill's music, directed the eleven-piece band in a funkified version of this traditional Methodist hymn, with horns and funk riffs from contemporary secular music. By the end, people were clapping, singing, and shouting. As he ran up the stairs, Bell declared "You have now been baptized in the funk," and from the reaction of the crowd, it appeared to be true.

Bell's sermon was from Psalm 34:14, "Turn from evil and do good; seek peace and pursue it." He preached on peace, but the sermon really answered the question, "What are you going to do with your energies?"

The range of his references was rhetorically impressive—he preached for forty minutes with few notes, a few props, and a fluid and passionate presentation—a virtuoso performance, especially when considering the breadth of the sermon. He moved from a quote about God's "fruitful becoming" by John Polkinghorne, the physicist turned Anglican preacher; to a video on how to pack a bullet; to a slide with a single reference, "Mother Teresa was 4'10" (showing that size doesn't matter relative to energy and power); to a picture of a little boy going out into a snow storm in underpants just to see how it feels; to the inner sanctum of a Lego store, which he compared to the wailing wall in Jerusalem; to the potent pictures of Tim Hetherington (the well-known photojournalist who died in Libya, covering the recent civil war); to Bergen-Belsen, and the story of how a supply of red lipstick was mistakenly brought to a group of female holocaust survivors who, in their ravaged state, put on the red lipstick and walked with pride—even as Bell explained that the human task is "to give back people's humanity—to go around handing out lipstick." The amalgamation of various ideas, media, and stories ended with a crescendo and with Bell imploring his listeners to focus their energies—to approach "a state of peaceful non-anxiousness" and to go out into the world and "give your energies and the best of yourself to the world." The audience clearly found it to be an exhilarating ride.

At the second service, I moved up to be closer to Bell and to the center stage. I immediately noticed that Carlton Cuse, the producer of the television series *Lost* and Bell's co-producer on his show *Stronger*, was sitting next to him. Cuse, who was raised Catholic, talked chummily to Bell the whole time, joining in the singing and listening intently to the sermon. After the second sermon, Bell saw me approaching him and said, "I hope that you don't think all megachurch pastors are jerks, now," making it clear, on a personal level, his interest in his audience and in people's responses.

The performance that he gave at Mars Hill was just that—a performance. But it was also a presentation that was real. In interviews with Bell, he discussed his thoughts on performance as it relates to what people call the "gospel," explaining, "I wanted to be a great communicator. That's all I cared about." Bell's college career as a budding and aspirational rock star was then, for him, a "warm-up" to his life as a communicator of the gospel—seeking out the largest audience possible.

Bell's passion for communicating is deeply intertwined with a feeling for what he calls the "gospel of Jesus," but his issue, from early on, was that the church itself seemed dull and lacking in the creativity that Bell had experienced in more "secular" forms of culture. "I was always fascinated with Jesus, but I always found the culture surrounding him, church sort of culture, less than vibrant. I didn't find it vital. Today there was the world with all of its pulsing energy and sort of electricity, and when I stepped into the Christian world, it was, how did you guys manage to unplug the thing?"[10]

This mix of fascination and a "mystical" sense of the presence of Jesus, which Bell described as "with him" even in the midst of his worst times in life, buoyed him despite experiences in church that were less than stimulating. This question of the gospel being "unplugged" from the current that Bell experienced in his own faith was echoed in the powerful relationship he has with his father, who would wonder out loud to his young son about the church, "It's supposed to better than this . . . it should be more beautiful, more compelling, smarter." And this passion to bring back the electricity into the church, Bell internalized, making it his mission to electrify the church with the experience of Jesus that he felt in his blood and bones.

Bell is a man unabashed in his adulation of other gifted performers, whether Ellen DeGeneres in her early comic routines, or Bono and U2, or Taylor Swift. He described how he had recently bought third row tickets to see Swift perform, "How does a 20-year-old fill an 11,000 seat Irvine arena? The art of it. The opening 30 seconds when she first came on stage, I'm still processing. How does she know to do that? It was genius."

Bell is also unreserved in his enthusiasm of great communicators. His early dream at seminary was to try and convince an evangelist, John Guest or Ed Dobson, to let him learn from them. He

---

10 Interview with Rob Bell by author, November 17, 2011.

offered, "Can I take out your trash? Just to follow you around. I had this sense, I want to follow somebody around who is mass communicating." Bell was charged by two equally compelling impulses, a love affair with Jesus and a passion to mass communicate. These impulses coalesced around the ministry, and starting a church that rejected traditional forms and engaged the senses on multiple levels, following his dad's injunction to create worship that would be more beautiful, smarter, and just as engaging as any secular form of communication.

Sensitive to the charge of hypocrisy and showboating, and defensive about the charge that one should only need to deliver the "word of God," Bell has faulted his accusers for falsifying the reality of what really happens in effective forms of communication, whether in the church or elsewhere. As he stated, "And what's interesting is, no one in pastor world would use the word performance. And there's all this sort of complete rubbish like, I don't know, I'll tell you where that church is going, because so and so is preaching the word. OK, there's a lot of churches where so and so is preaching the word that aren't [growing], OK, that person, she's a performer, just say it. She knows how to preach the word. You know what I mean?"[11]

Bell is quite aware of how certain kinds of "dull" communication styles are excused by pastors who say, "Yes, I just preach the word," rationalizing why they draw no one into their churches. His words of admiration and his deep investment in perfecting forms of communication and performance flowed like a line of cocaine through nearly every one of our conversations.

"It almost feels like you're more in love with just the process of communication than with whatever you want to call it, the gospel," I noted in an interview with Bell. For the only time in our ten hours of interviews, Bell stopped talking. After a long pause, "That's a really compelling insight." He said, "My experience, I had seen people talking about the gospel, preaching the gospel, being true to the gospel, and it sucked."

---

11 Interview with Rob Bell by author, November 19, 2011.

He then continued to describe various (unnamed) ministers thrust into the pulpit, either out of guilt or because their father left the pulpit to them. Others preachers "preach the word" out of obligation, compulsion, or "fear of God." Their sharing the gospel, Bell suggested, undercuts their witness and "empties" their ability to engage their listeners.

In contrast, Bell realized that "the people who love it the most, and who have the most impact for the gospel seem to just do what they love and throw themselves into it, and don't spend a lot of time telling you how committed they are to the gospel, and how much they are being true to Jesus' call." For Bell, allowing the energy of the spirit to flow is critical to whether his communication is effective and authentic. And for him this translates into a primary communication principle: one must *show rather than tell.* As he said, "I never give a state-of-the-church sermon. I don't explain a theory of biblical interpretation; I interpret the scriptures, and I give pictures of where the church should go."

The good news of the gospel is a lived condition of flesh and blood; for Bell to abstract the message and to use it as a hammer or threat is not only a failure in modes of communication but also a distortion of what he takes as the "truth" of the gospel. Critics of Bell often accuse him of avoiding the hard claims of doctrine and dogma, and this may or may not be true. Yet while belief may secure certainty at one level of abstraction, Bell argues that to concretize this truth misses how the truth is lived out both in the self and in relation to others and the community at large. If he does avoid the hard claims of dogma, it's intentional.

The charge of hypocrisy is one Bell hears frequently. And he makes the same charge, at least implicitly, against fellow preachers of the word who either are damaged by guilt or are victims of a God who is (as he says) "a bastard"—a God who seems anxious to send people to hell, a God whose interest is as a moral police officer, a God whose first impulse is to punish, a God who needs followers who don't talk back.

Bell's God, on the other hand, is anything but a traditional Calvinist TULIP God who has predestined some to heaven and some to hell, a God who depends not on human choice but on his own sovereign will and whose plan includes an inescapable end in which those who are not chosen are to be damned to hell forever—and for God's glory. This God is not Bell's God. For Bell, getting belief right is much less important than experiencing an active love for oneself, love of and for one's God, and for others.

Bell takes his understanding of God's character from the life and teachings of Jesus. God is like the father in the Luke 15 narrative, who, rather than demanding a changed heart and mind from his wayward son, runs to embrace the prodigal and to welcome him home. Bell believes in a God who seeks to bring all people to God— inviting followers to join and partner with God in the creation and recreation of the world. Bell may be play-acting in order to communicate the full range of this good news, but he believes this acting comes out as a result of an incarnated energy given by God and disclosed in Jesus. The art of communication for him is not a masking process but an unveiling and empowering event of the incarnated God in Christ, seeking partners in the salvation of the world.

But in the midst of this glory of the gospel and the sharing of the good news, questions linger. Some have complained that Bell's time in the spotlight is up. That his charisma has passed. And maybe that is the fate or the fear of every celebrity—Can I keep this going? Have I lost the magic? The story of the rise and fall of *Nooma* is one of those stories. How Bell deals with failure is just as important as how he negotiates success.

The End of Nooma

Nooma, as a product, hangs in the balance—but, at least for Bell, it's over. Most startups fail, but the *Nooma* videos have sold more units than any other book or film Bell has made. In 2010, 2.5 million *Noomas* had been sold worldwide, and the actual number of people who have watched these short films may be far larger. It is reported, for instance, that 99 percent of *Nooma* viewers recommend it to others and that more than half of those who watch the films make some kind of "life-changing decision."[12] The original contract with Bell was to make 32 films, but there are only 24 in existence and Bell will make no more. Therein lies a story.

The original impetus for this innovative media was MTV. MTV was interested in someone who could respond to their market's "high interest in Jesus" and "disinterest in church," but they also wanted somebody who would do a show about "all religions." Bell didn't fit; he cared about Jesus but not about other religions. People recognized Bell's talents early on, and like the nearly instant crowds that gathered at the "Shed," the euphemism used to describe the Mars Hill church mall building, interest in Bell as a potential media star percolated from the start of the new church.

The MTV connection was short-lived, but a small group of motivated and talented people gathered around Bell to communicate the "brilliance" of what they heard on Sundays at the Shed. "We didn't know what we were doing . . . maybe there will be an MTV format. . . . It kind of morphed into these films. Because Rob said, "I got stuff." We thought they were going to be 30-45 minutes. We shot tons of film, throwing money away like it's water, and ended up with a 12 minute film with all the cuts and edits. We're screwed; because everything is a 22-minute format, at least for television. Which is where we thought we were going."[13]

In the beginning, then, no one knew exactly what they were up to, but this small group knew Bell was saying things no one else was talking about in ways that people who had no interest in religion or church would listen. They were right about *Nooma*, as an early supporter proclaimed, "And it turned out to be, I think, one of the

---

12 See Steve Carr's interview about *Nooma* and Flannel's plans in *The Christian Post*, Church & Ministries, December, 11 2010.

http://www.christianpost.com/news/interview-steve-carr-on-frustrations-with-the-churchfrancis-chanfilms-48024/page2.html. Accessed November 16, 2011.

13 Interview with Rob Bell associate by author, November 19, 2011.

coolest, not as in avant garde cool, but one of the most interesting ways to communicate the gospel without a hard sell—which is to start conversations about what your life would be like, instead of let's all hold hands and say the sinners prayer. What would it be like if we would just think about living a different way?"[14]

Bell's style of showing rather than telling fit smoothly into the short films he created. Each *Nooma* had a one-word title and themes that were both universal to the human condition and particular to situations that nearly anyone might encounter. This short list gives a taste of their range:

- "Flames," (the integration of spirituality and sexuality);
- "She," (the feminine force of God);
- "Luggage," (the baggage of old hurts that need forgiveness);
- "Rhythm," (focusing on each choice as a way to tune one's relationship to God);
- "Store," (dealing with anger in more creative and constructive ways);
- "Name," (overcoming how people always compare themselves to others);
- "Shells," (on the importance of saying no);
- "Corner," (on how in saving another, people save themselves);
- and the last, "Whirlwind," which we will explore shortly.

Bell, along with others, invested his own savings in the production of the *Nooma* films. Flannel, the Christian nonprofit that produced them, continued to support Bell creatively through the production of his films, as well as in the design and production of his first three books, *Velvet Elvis: Repainting the Christian Faith* (2005), *Sex God: Exploring the Endless Connections between Sexuality and Spirituality* (2007), and *Jesus Wants to Save Christians: A Manifesto for the*

---

14 Interview with Rob Bell associate by author, November 19, 2011.

Church in Exile (2008). Flannel teamed with Zondervan, a Christian publishing house, to design Bell's first four books.[15] As time went on, outside investors also contributed heavily to Flannel, and the need to raise funds often fell on Bell as the "star" in the enterprise. The internal workings of Flannel, however, highlighted a part of Bell's work and artistic philosophy that reveal a great deal about him as a charismatic leader. The core group of designers and creatives were talented individuals who later started a successful advertising company. With *Nooma*, the "team" wanted to make a film that could compete with anything on MTV. They also wanted to innovate in ways no one had yet seen. They weren't necessarily religious or even Christian. Several were agnostics of one type or another, with little concern about evangelism, especially not the forms used by evangelicals in the recent past. They just wanted to make something beautiful and engaging.

More than anyone else, Bell supported this process and these individuals all the way. For him, what is good, true, and beautiful is *not* limited to "Christian" artists, designers, or thinkers. The subversive side of Bell chafed against the Christian media ghetto—products that screamed Christian content and the "right" message.

This willingness to push against the edges of acceptable evangelical principles of thought and art began the slow demise of his relationship with Flannel and eventually with Zondervan—perhaps even to the larger, evangelical Christian community. And as Bell began to explore wider and larger realms of theological interpretations of scripture and ethics, he became the object of outright suspicion.

Internal conflicts and firings at Flannel shifted loyalties, and in 2009, the Flannel board began to swing to a more conservative theological make-up. This movement produced tensions and cracks in the working relationships, severing a team that created one of the

---

15 In 1988 Zondervan became an arm of HarperCollins; Zondervan, conveniently, is also located in Grandville, Michigan, the site, of course, of Mars Hill Bible Church.

most popular forms of media the Christian world had ever experienced. At one point, as one of Bell's associates explained to me, the director of Flannel deadpanned, referring to Bell's fifteen minutes of fame, "Rob's at 14:45 and ticking." Bell's associate defended Bell, but the writing was on the wall. Bell's relationship with Flannel came to an inglorious end.

Another close associate of Bell's, having come to Flannel in the last years of Bell's affiliation, was witness to many of the tensions of the final break. As a designer, he was a part of a group that went to Los Angeles to meet and investigate the possibility of turning to Francis Chan, a rising evangelical author and popular preacher, for a new series that came to be entitled *Basics*, as a part of an expanding range of offerings for Flannel. As the board became more conservative, Flannel took a new direction, seeing Chan as a way to "balance" Bell's more freewheeling style that asked questions where many conservatives wanted answers.

For Bell, the idea of balance was anathema. Since Bell maintained a creative veto on the development of the *Nooma* films, the films stopped as he ended his relationship with Flannel. The contract for 32 films was never fulfilled. This "breach" ended the relationship. For Bell supporters, this had much more to do with Bell's integrity and his determination to stand up for what he believed. Needless to say, Flannel thought differently.

This new theological balance—toward a more conservative theology—seemed to Bell to be a direct attack on his vision. This balance translated into a more traditional evangelical worldview that would use veiled threats and fear in bringing people to God. And the first installment of Chan's *Basics*, indeed, marks that shift. It's for a reason that his first video was entitled, "Fear God."

To balance Bell, Flannel brought in Chan as a more conservative evangelical who expressed the need to know that the threat of hell is real, biblical, and a legitimate way to "encourage" others to come to God. And once Bell's book, *Love Wins*, came out, Francis Chan threw down the gauntlet in direct response to Bell's work: "Jesus chose strong and terrifying language when He spoke of hell . . . I believe His intention was to stir a fear in us that would cause us to take hell seriously and avoid it at all costs."[16]

To one of Bell's friends whom I interviewed, this contrast was not a balance. Instead, it was the very thing this friend had grown to "despise" about the Reformed Church—its dogmatic and unrelenting moral puritanism as well as the not so implicit fear that "bound" people rather than set them "free." Commenting on the subject, this friend recalled the following events: "So I went on this thing to meet Francis and to talk about the project, and immediately after that I went to *Poets, Profits, and Preachers*. I got back from Los Angeles on a Saturday, and then PPP started on Sunday night and went through like Wednesday and I quit Flannel on the following Thursday, the day after PPP."[17]

The break in the relationship also had to do with the 2008 release of *Jesus Wants to Save Christians*. In this book, Bell waded into deep waters, challenging Christians with the "God of the oppressed," and with forms of liberation theology that did not sit well with the more theologically and politically conservative Flannel board. On the back of the book, Bell wrote, "Did you know a church just completed a 20 million dollar building improvement at the same time it was reported that 20 percent of Grand Rapids lives in poverty."

One of Bell's most ardent supporters announced, "I hated that book." When asked why, he explained, "I think there are better ways to move the kingdom forward than to piss off somebody you don't have to piss off." Bell's move in the direction of what his friend described as a "Green God" was far from universally embraced.[18]

Bell's political theology was no longer a quirky and creative portrayal of Jesus as the one who sets people free to love, forgive, and

---

16 See Francis Chan's and Preston Sprinkle's *erasing hell: what God said about eternity, and the things we've made up.* Colorado Springs, CO: David C. Cook, 2011, p. 86.

17 Interview with Rob Bell associate by author, November 18, 2011.

18 Interview with Rob Bell associate by author, November 19, 2011.

serve. It began to shift to a theology that called into question many of the typical ways megachurches and mainstream evangelicalism went about their business. Was it okay to spend all your time as a church calling people to salvation while the people in your town were living in dank, dark neighborhoods with poor schools, dangerous housing, and inadequate food? For Bell, it was no longer about a simple evangelical message, if it ever was. Instead, it came to be about the subversion of typical church models, not only in terms of aesthetic and liturgical innovations but also in how the local church should actually operate in and with its community.

By the last installment of *Nooma*, the writing was on the wall. *Whirlwind* has all the typical qualities of the other *Nooma* films, but its stripped down vision is even more extreme. It opens with the usual background music, gentle and melodic, showing an empty, two-lane road as a dark figure is seen in the distance; the street is framed on both sides by dark shadows; there is an empty wooded field and a grey sky; it is a cold, dank winter. And then, the figure approaches. It's Bell, sober and intense. As he approaches the camera, he begins to tell an "old, old story, about a man named Job, one of the oldest stories ever told."

Bell quickly narrates the story of Job, the good man, and his family—the acquisition of wealth, success, and happiness, and then the crushing loss of it all. Job loses his wealth. His children are killed. He's sitting in ashes, and his wife lashes out, "Are you still holding onto your integrity? Curse God and die." Job's friends come, and they all take turns giving explanations. Then, in the midst of recounting the peak of Job's problems, Bell interjects, "And that is what we all want, explanations, isn't it? And they all debate, discuss and discuss, and then in the end, when everybody has had a time to speak, God speaks."

From there, Bell recites the questions God asks of Job from chapters 38 and 39. It is, once again, a virtuoso performance; words tumble from Bell, question after question after question. He quotes God, at once profound and accusatory, asking: "What is the way to the abode of light? And where does darkness reside? Can you take them to their places? Do you know the paths to their dwellings?" (Job 38:19-20).

Bell then brings in Job's response. "I am unworthy—how can I reply to you? . . . I spoke once . . . but I will say no more (Job 41:4-5). Bell then concludes,

> We want answers. We want explanations. We want to know why we suffer, and there are times the only honest, healthy, human thing is to shout your question, rage against heaven and demand an explanation. But true wisdom knows when to speak and when to be silent, because your story is not over. The last word has not been spoken, and there may be way more going on here than any of us realize. And so may you be released from having to always understand why everything happens the way it does, and may this freedom open you up to all sorts of new perspectives. And may you have the wisdom to say, "I spoke once, but I will say no more."

The last line of *Whirlwind,* as one of Bell's associates recalled, was a very appropriate last line for the *Nooma* film series itself. Bell's relationship with *Nooma* was broken, and he would speak for them no more.

In *Whirlwind,* however, Bell's charismatic bond is on full display. The story is not finished: the empathy with those who suffer, the valleys we all face, and new life rising always from the ashes of the old. Bell's story certainly would begin a new chapter, with a twist no one saw coming. Not only would Bell end his relationship with *Nooma,* but in the not too distant future, he would be leaving Mars Hill— seeking his next creative act. The story does not end.

Bell lived through his own sense of betrayal at the hands of the very organization he had started. Flannel went in another direction. Friends had been fired, and associates turned on him. The takeaway for Bell was not bitterness or accusations. It is, as he consistently says in all sorts of venues, that the story is not done; your story, our story, my story is not done.

Bell acts again as proxy to new life, to life coming out of death. This is what the successful charismatic bond is built on: a figure who takes a common and recognizable mess and frames it in poetic and moving words, calling forth a transcendental vision to a new horizon. Only God knows, and we as readers and onlookers discern, if this way is true, but with Bell the future lies open. He is walking on down the road.

chapter four

CANVAS

"To him, all good things—trout as well as eternal salvation—come by grace and grace comes by art and art does not come easy." [1]

Norman Maclean, A River Runs Through It

Every artist needs time, the rough edges of reality, and inspiration to make their work come alive. They also need a canvas. And Bell's canvas has been Mars Hill church, where he created a perspective, repainted the faith, dabbled in media, and performed his way to a style and strategy of preaching that many copy, study, and admire—and some despise. But this wasn't always so. In Bell's first sermon at Mars Hill on February 7, 1999,[2] he set up the biblical precedent for his church's mission to communicate the gospel in ways that people in contemporary culture could hear and understand. Bell frames the sermon around Paul's speech to the Greeks on Mars Hill in Acts 17, where Paul appeals to the Greeks whom he perceives as worship-

---

1 See Norman Maclean's *A River Runs Through It, and Other Stories*, Chicago, IL: University of Chicago Press, 1976, p. 5.

2 Listen to Rob Bell's first sermon at Mars Hill church, February 7, 1999, at: http://www.box.com/shared/l15eieakxe. Accessed February 13, 2012.

ping God without knowing God. All of Bell's rhetorical and oratorical tricks of the trade are present. But absent is his artistic gift for maintaining tensions in the ambiguities of texts, the ability to rend artistic flourish from complex biblical stories, and the capacity to synthesize the divine matrix of creation behind the typical binaries of the sacred and the profane. What we hear, rather, is a preacher in the demagogic vein of megachurch pastors like Mark Driscoll.[3]

Bell's first sermon exhibits the naiveté of a powerful young speaker, deeply certain of the righteousness of his cause. The easy condemnations are all there: the "satanic" labeling of Star Wars, the quick judgments of entertainers, the categorizing of all other gods as "satanic idols," the assumption that "sin" is the only thing Jesus sees when he grieves for Jerusalem. This is the Driscoll-like preacher who hits all the right notes, cracking jokes and making clever asides. A pastor who assumes that if you don't get it or you don't bring your Bible to church, the joke is on you. This kind of demagoguery tempts many and is attractive to those who want to make simple distinctions between what is good and what is evil—and even more powerfully, who is in and who is not.

In the more mature, later version of Bell, we find a human being who has come into his own through battles over the equality of women in leadership, through his own personal demons and "shadow," and through engagement with biblical texts that avoid the simple distinctions between good and evil and between labeling who is "in" and who is "out." Bell consistently speaks of "stripping away" the clutter to get to the essence of the thing itself. Rather than avoiding complexity, he makes complexity pliant and pregnant with meaning. And in his last sermon to Mars Hill in 2011, Bell makes clear that while grace is simple, communicating grace is hard "because it costs

---

3 Mark Driscoll is founder and pastor of Mars Hill Church in Seattle, a 9,000 member church started in 1997; the two like-named churches have traveled in quite distinct ways since their foundings. Driscoll's critique of Bell as a "syncretist" is quite revealing, not so much about Bell, whom Driscoll does not know, but about himself. http://www.youtube.com/watch?v=1BaPFGhFO1o&feature =related. Accessed February13, 2012.

something. Because it only exists as a result of your sweat and blood, you have a visceral attachment to it. It came out of you, and when it's completed, you may be exhausted, spent and ready for a rest, but you are exhilarated."[4]

As Norman MacLean testifies, all these things, "come by grace, and grace comes by art, and art does not come easy." Bell's artistry on the canvas of Mars Hill did not come easy, but the results catapulted him into places few preachers go. In order to get at and communicate this gospel, one suffers. We see this in Bell's story as he went to places he did not want to go, not only within himself but also in the biblical text, discovering grace for himself and for those who listened to him. We also catch moments of dramatic intellectual and spiritual conversions that shifted his perspective and deepened his own understanding of the Bible and the faith, setting him on a path that would bring him up against his own evangelical conventions and eventually put him at odds with the larger evangelical world.

The Early Bell Converted

From the beginning, Bell caught people with his wit and humor. He opened his first sermon at Mars Hill with these lines: "If you did not bring a Bible; this is a Bible church, which means we read our. . . Bible. Three of you are on target here. [laughter] We will begin on Acts 17. I'm starting a new series this morning. [big laughter] Some of you are thinking, 'I have not heard that guy preach a bad sermon in this church.' [bigger laughter]" Even lighthearted, Bell was dead serious. He worked with humor in order to let his listeners know that he meant business. They should be ready to listen to him preach with a Bible in their hand, just as he held one in his. For Bell, this church was going places, and listeners were either on board or not.

---

4 Sermon, "Rob Bell's Parting Epistle to Mars Hill: "Grace + Peace," 12.19.2011. In *Sojourners: Faith in Action for Social Justice,* Cathleen Falsani. http://sojo.net/blogs/2011/12/19/rob-bells-parting-epistle-mars-hill-grace-peace. Accessed January 5, 2012.

It was a remarkable bit of chutzpah—a brand new church, a preacher who had never given a series of sermons. Elders at Calvary Church warned him that he'd be lucky to have 100 members at the end of his first year, even as Bell faced a packed room and more than 1,000 people in the two services on his inaugural Sunday at Mars Hill church.

In his first sermon, Bell fancied himself like Paul speaking in the Areopagus, staring down his cultured despisers and pagan god lovers. But, as we know, his crowd in Grand Rapids was hardly pagan or godless. Bell spoke to a crowd that was drawn to a 28-year-old, fiery Bible preacher with wit, good looks, and a sense of humor, minus the liturgical and dogmatic Reformed trappings. Bell had them eating out of his hands. And in that first sermon, Bell dug deeply into his own visceral experiences, painting the Bible as a real and living story.

> In Athens, while Paul is waiting for his partners in the gospel, he's distressed to see the city full of idols. Athens was the center of philosophy of the ancient Near East—where Plato got his start and Aristotle got his start. Every building that was built would be in the honor of a false god, basically a satanic idol of some sort. They did not have a Bible-preaching, Jesus-loving church in Athens. So Paul comes into a city where everything is dedicated to the rejection of God, and he is distressed—extreme, gut-wrenching distress.

This was the early Bell, completely certain of his gospel, like Paul, seeing idols and sin where God and righteousness should be. Bell was not looking to find grace in the midst of *this* culture, or see how truth, beauty, and goodness may have been lurking behind the scenes. He wanted a Jesus-loving, Bible church. He went on to describe a scene at a concert he attended, which piqued this righteous young preacher: "When the concert reached its climax [the singer] has 12,000 young people of my generation screaming profanities at the top of their lungs, and they're enjoying it. Have you ever had that feeling where you are overwhelmed and distressed at the sin of the world?"

So Bell, in his best Pauline prophetic moment, judged and condemned this worldliness. And out of his own distress and passion he called for salvation of his generation from sin. This is the classic evangelical "burden of the gospel." He wanted to pull out as many "sinners" as he could from this sinking ship. Bell's early talent was on full display—self-confidence, humor, detailed stories, and the ability to weave biblical and contemporary portraits with smooth, even elegant, transitions. He had the crowd.

And yet, in many ways, Bell missed much of what Paul was after. Paul, in fact, was admitting that the Greeks indeed were worshipping God, and just didn't know it—hence their shrines "To an Unknown God" (Acts 17:23). Paul was arguing, in essence, that there are truths in non-Christian religions and philosophies, just not the complete truth. Bell wasn't there yet.

But in these early years as he was famously preaching through the book of Leviticus, Bell experienced as he explained in interviews, "an intellectual conversion." A group of Messianic Jews, along with some Dutch Calvinists, introduced Bell to the Jewish roots movement, discovering the Jewish background of Jesus' thought and life. As he explained, "Oh my goodness, oh yeah, it was massive, I actually feel like that turned my faith around. Kristen, my wife would say, that that's 'when things went from black and white to color.' I would say that, yeah, the Bible became, oh my word, fascinating, it became real."[5]

Bell was introduced to the lifestyle and rituals of the messianic Jewish movement, which fascinated but also concerned him, since he could see in them a kind of "reverse legalism" that he wanted to avoid. Nonetheless, the power of the movement and the thinking anchored and illumined the reality behind the language and actions of the early Jesus community. "The Jewish heritage does ground you. I remember when I realized it in 1999. Jesus didn't talk about getting

---

5 Interview with Rob Bell by author, March 28, 2012.

people somewhere else. When Jesus spoke of eternal life, it was about a renewed creation; this world is our home." [6]

Bell's early passion did not change with this intellectual and spiritual conversion. In fact, the energy of this shift stimulated Bell all the more. Over the course of his career, nearly all of his intellectual and media projects had their roots in these early transformations. Indeed, throughout the next twelve years, Bell's fissionable energy to share and offer the gospel remained. In fact, it deepened. His growth, however, was *not* toward a liberal interreligious cosmopolitanism, but rather to a more complex view of Christianity and its relationship with its founding religious culture—Judaism. For Bell, the this-worldly nature of the Jewish community inspired him to begin to "repaint" the faith and to see the power of Christ's "new creation" in its ability to change this world, motivating him even more strongly to make disciples of Jesus Christ for the sake of *this* world.[7]

Practicing an Art of Opposites

The result of Bell's transformations made their impact early on at Mars Hill. By the 2005 publication of his first book, *Velvet Elvis*, his "repainting" of the Christian faith was well on its way. The shift toward gender inclusion; interpreting scripture as story rather than as some kind of inerrant document; the prioritizing of experience over belief; the emphasis on discipleship for the sake of the here and now—each of these became the pivot points for Bell's notion of a church as a "catalyst for the kingdom of God," transformed by Christ's presence and ready to serve the poor of the world.

---

6 A key text for Bell during this time was David Bivin's and Roy Blizzard, Jr.'s *Understanding the Difficult Words of Jesus: New Insights From a Hebrew Perspective* Shippensburg, PA: Destiny Image Publishers, 1994.

7 Bell explained to me that one of the most important books for him during these early years at Mars Hill was Dallas Willard's *The Divine Conspiracy: Rediscovering our Hidden Life in God.* NY: HarperCollins Publishing Inc., 1998. Willard, a Southern Baptist and professional philosopher, emphasizes the direct discipleship of Jesus Christ and the study and practice of knowing the kingdom of God for the sake of this world.

Andrew Crouch describes a radical vision of what Bell and his wife Kristen thought about the Bible. Bell, in his tendency to hype each new development, explained, "This is not just the same old message with new methods; we're rediscovering Christianity as an Eastern religion, as a way of life. Legal metaphors for faith don't deliver a way of life. We grew up in churches where people knew the nine verses why we don't speak in tongues, but had never experienced the overwhelming presence of God."[8] Bell, who knew this old-time evangelical message like the back of his hand and who had preached these evangelical sermons, moved forcefully to rethink his faith and tradition. Experience of Christ trumped intellectual belief in doctrine; fresh questions and real doubts undermined rote memorization and parroted lines; the felt presence of God liberated one from dry declarations and cliché Christian worship; mystical awareness of God's kingdom triumphed over pining for a heaven to come; and an openness to the art of opposites and comfort with tensions challenged legal declarations of true and false, right and wrong, good and evil.

In 2004, at the height of his evangelical popularity, Bell rejected the literal tradition of biblical interpretation. He declared the impossibility of reading the Bible as an inerrant text, stating that the Bible invited and demanded interpretation. In fact, the idea of the Bible as simply a manual of truth, according to Bell, was "warped and toxic."[9] To believe that we can "just teach the Bible" is not only impossible, but a myth, and to think that the Bible's meaning is plain and undistorted by bias is false. Like a newfound convert, Bell ran with this new knowledge: "The Bible has to be interpreted. Decisions have to made about what it means now, today."[10]

---

8 See Andrew Crouch's "The Emergent Mystique," *Christianity Today*, November 1, 2004. http://www.christianitytoday.com/ct/2004/november/12.36.html. Accessed on July 9, 2012.
9 Rob Bell, *Velvet Elvis*, p. 53.
10 Rob Bell, *Velvet Elvis*, p. 55.

He turned away from the early twentieth century Christian fundamentalist tradition. Fundamentalism itself had rejected the nineteenth-century European attempt to look at Christian scriptures as historical documents. This so-called attack on faith galvanized a whole tradition of Christian fundamentalists who defined scripture as inerrant and, more importantly, a word that can be plainly understood by any common sense reader of the Bible. Preachers claimed that they preached the "Word of God" alone and that this word was perfect in every way, historically, scientifically, morally, and theologically. The crux of the claim put the Bible above interpretation and above critique.

For Bell in 2005, the writing was literally on the page. Bell argued that he had discovered the Christian faith "as a way of life." This meant, as he explained, "foundationalism died." The epistemological assertion that the eye and the mind can see reality, and even the Bible, without filter, without prejudice, without a cultural framework, was false at its core. Cultural biases frame the way we see, speak, and read. By definition, we understand the gospel, as such, only through our linguistic and perceptual senses.

And with this insight, Bell's early certainty died. A newfound humility arose; he "discovered the Bible as a human product," and Kristen, his wife, joined him on this journey, "I grew up thinking that we've figured out the Bible . . . that we knew what it means. Now I have no idea what most of it means. And yet I feel like life is big again—like life used to be black and white, and now it's in color."[11]

The liberating nature of this discovery may have been revolutionary to the Bells, but its origins for many Christians started two centuries earlier in the work and theology of Frederich Schleiermacher, the father of Protestant liberalism and the writer of the classic *On Religion: Speeches to its Cultured Despisers.*[12] Like Schleiermacher,

---

11 See Andrew Crouch's "The Emergent Mystique."
12 See Friedrich Schleiermacher's, *On Religion: Speeches to its Cultured Despisers.* Cambridge, Translated by Richard Crouter; originally published in 1799 [1996].

Bell retrieved the religious experience as the ultimate touchstone for the Christian faith, and the Bible as its witness and inspiration.

For Bell, however, not only was the introduction to Jesus' Jewishness critical, but also key was Dallas Willard's bracing notion that discipleship trumped belief and dogma as the touchstone of Christian faithfulness. Brian McLaren was yet another critical influence. In the late 1990s, McLaren and numerous other edgy leaders generated the Emergent church movement within American evangelical Christianity. In the same 2004 article, the Bells named McLaren's early work *A New Kind of Christian*, as their lodestar.[13] Remarkably, it's the last time that Bell mentions McLaren. Ever careful to avoid Christian labels, Bell, thereafter, refused any identification with the Emergent movement—one more sign of his allergy to identifying himself with any of the nascent Christian subcultures.

Even so, the Emergent movement shadowed Bell's work. Many accused Bell of being derivative; his insights were a function not only of McLaren's thinking but of Protestant liberalism more generally. Bell, ever careful, refused not only the Emergent church label, but more particularly rejected the notion that he was a Protestant liberal. These old labels "bored" him and in fact "missed the whole point."

But the question lingered and remains even now: Is Bell bringing a liberal Protestant Trojan Horse into the house of Reformed American evangelicalism? The answer is complex, but on its face, it's a resounding no. For Bell, the closed-minded nature of liberalism is as much a problem as the myopic sensibilities of many on the conservative side of Protestantism. Bell, like a good radical empiricist,[14] embraces the whole of reality, the possibility of dimensions that are neither seen nor counted but that can be intuited and experienced

---

13 See Brian McLaren's *A New Kind of Christian: A Tale of Two Friends on a Spiritual Journey*. San Francisco: CA, Jossey-Bass, 2001.

14 The American philosopher, William James, developed the tradition of radical empiricism; he defined the "full facts" of experience, including religious experience, as "a conscious field plus its object as felt or thought of plus an attitude towards the object plus the sense of a self to whom the attitude belongs . . ." In *Varieties of Religious Experience*. NY: Penguin Books, 1982, p. 393.

through their effects in the real world. Bell remains open to the miraculous in the midst of the every day. In his work, whenever he comes up against conundrums of human stubbornness or rationalists who deny the potential of divine intervention, he goes back to the core claims of the gospel that the "tomb is empty, and Christ is risen." These aren't the usual marks of a liberal rationalist.

When confronted with labels of liberalism, his response has been:

> Two weeks ago, we had communion at Mars Hill and people get down on their knees and serve each other, including people with cancer, and some in wheelchairs. People are serving and praying and healing one another; a whole cosmos is created in those gestures and that's beautiful. We're gathering around an ancient, strange ritual, where we take the bread and cup and tell the story of God loving every single person, death being conquered, and new creation coming alive right here in our midst. And that's as particular as the resurrection and as miraculous as the empty tomb; we're okay with the wild and mysterious and miraculous, and that's not a pre-rational, magical, and mythical unicorn party. We're fully aware of evidence, and we're aware of the scientific method, and we know that Newton wrote some things about the mechanical laws of the universe. We just think that the universe may be a little more open than that. And that's a beautiful thing.

Neither a foundationalist nor a fundamentalist, Bell has a different core: The life, death, and resurrection of Jesus Christ are as close to him as any Christian doctrine or belief. For him, the movement of loss and life, and the death and resurrection of Jesus are the very latticework upon which he builds his life, faith, and hope—the realities that correspond to what he has experienced in his own life and in thousands of lives of those with whom he has ministered.

More pointedly, Bell has said that conservative evangelicals who claim that the gospel saved their soul and left the world behind have corrupted the church and undercut what should be its central message—the "reclamation of culture." The mission of Mars Hill would be the working out of salvation in "fear and trembling," and the empowering of people to be healed and trained to love others and serve the least and the lost. God's presence is as real to Bell as is "his own breath," as he has said repeatedly. How Bell would make these claims plausible and powerful is the story of his artistry and its evolving, persuasive power.

Collapsing the Sacred and the Profane

The old distinctions between Christian and non-Christian, sacred and secular, no longer make sense, as Bell exclaimed: "It was like a giant exercise in missing the point." If God creates "the world and everything in it," as the scripture proclaims, then the traditional evangelical distinction makes no sense at all. This insight led him to declare that the whole world is sacred, alive with spirit, and must now be reclaimed in Christ. God the Creator looks for "co-creators," men and women who will join God in reclaiming the world through new creation made possible in the life, death, and resurrection of Jesus Christ. It parallels what the artist does, taking the common, everyday world and stripping away excess to allow others to see the simple beauty of the thing as it is.

Existence becomes sacred. Art is the task of making the common sacred, making the everyday a sacrament, understanding that Jesus' very ministry to the least and the poor embodies this very principle that in Christ all things are blessed—the rich, the poor, the beautiful, the ugly. All things become sacred, and all human beings, no matter their value, reflect the very image of God.

Bell's early work on the book of Leviticus and his fascination with the traditions of the Jews, including the Hebrew Bible and rabbinic teachings, helped him to penetrate the central transformative turn in the Jesus movement. He insists in his sermon, "Christ in the Commons," that Leviticus 10:10 sets out the primary mechanism by which the Mosaic covenant is established—the instruction and ordinances are given for the formation of God's tabernacle with God's people, "so that you can distinguish between the holy and the common, between the unclean and the clean." Here, we have the basis not only of Judaism but of the whole theory of religion, that religion creates distinctions between the sacred and the profane, the clean and the unclean, the good and the evil.

This series of distinctions captures how Israel functioned as a community of faith—a social movement that has a sacred center. And, it constructs the very terms that social scientists have used to describe religion.[15] Bell attacks the heart of this distinction. He argues that the Jesus revolution collapses the distinctions between the sacred and profane. The Christ event shatters these divisions, announcing the sacred nature of the creation in all its color and glory.

At the same time, Bell acknowledges the concept of sin, but its existence in no way diminishes the divine stamp on reality. Sin may distort our most sacred human intentions, but the very notion of secularity is a consequence of the misleading lens of religion, a kind of interpretive sin in which the human eye is blurred and blinded. Nonetheless, sin is not merely ignorance, but it is overcome by a paradigmatic shift in and through the resurrection of Jesus Christ who dies for sin, has victory over death, and reclaims creation as God's domain.

In Bell's thought, the declaration in Jesus' response to the Pharisees inaugurates the core constitution of this revolution. In Matthew 12:3-8, the Pharisees accuse Jesus and his disciples of breaking the law on the Sabbath:

---

15 These insights are at the heart of the key models of religion in the twentieth century. Emile Durkheim, the father of the sociological study of religion, argued that the sacred and profane was the very core of religion. Mircea Eliade, the father of religious studies, wrote his most read book, *The Sacred and Profane: The Nature of Religion,* to explain his understanding of the religious life. The power of this theme underlies much of the philosophical debates over how to interpret forms of secularism within modern life. Modern life assumes the distinction between the sacred and the secular.

[Jesus] answered, "Haven't you read what David did when he and his companions were hungry? He entered the house of God, and he and his companions ate the consecrated bread— which was not lawful for them to do, but only for the priests. Or haven't you read in the Law that the priests on Sabbath duty in the temple desecrate the Sabbath and yet are innocent? I tell you that something greater than the temple is here. If you had known what these words mean, 'I desire mercy, not sacrifice,' you would not have condemned the innocent. For the Son of Man is Lord of the Sabbath."

In this passage, Jesus throws down the gauntlet; he argues, in the spirit of the Hebrew prophetic tradition, that mercy and the spirit trump the law and obedience. Bell explains that in the context of the Hebrew tradition, Jesus' pronouncement breaks the central proposition that controls Jewish thought, that the law puts a "fence" around the sacred and stipulates what is good and bad, sacred and profane. Jesus disrupts this whole notion. Bell argues that religion, so-called, distorts the nature of Jesus' work and makes everyone blind when it separates and divides reality as sacred and profane.

This comes out in Bell's frontal attack against the notion within Protestantism that some are called to be "missionaries" who go out from churches to proclaim the gospel and serve others. For Bell this whole movement distorts the universal Christian vocation that all are called as ministers; all are "ambassadors of reconciliation." Motivationally, missionaries undermine the radical nature of the Christian calling—all occupations are, by nature, sacred tasks.

Bell probes, "Why not have commissioning services for teachers, for business people? Not to do so disempowers those who are not doing mission work, so-called." Bell suggests that each person— whether business person, artist, teacher, or mechanic—is doing the work of making or creating something, and this very act of creation parallels and participates in the action of the Creator who started the whole world moving from the beginning.

Art Making

Bell is well aware that most people don't consider a sermon an art form nor preachers artists. As he deadpanned in his 2009 seminar, "Poets, Prophets, and Preachers," "For most people, the sermon is boring and insipid . . . a form of propaganda; the building must be built . . . a sermon in service of something else." From here, Bell set out an audacious goal: to "reclaim the ancient and beautiful art of preaching." The five talks lay out his philosophy of preaching, beginning with a passionate motivation that as a preacher, "I should have fire in my bones, I can't hold it in."

Bell believes sermons let the word become flesh and have the "power to create new worlds." This "fresh word" begins with a premise, "Where and how you begin the story and where and how you end the story shapes and determines what you're telling." For Bell, the proper beginning is in Genesis 1 and 2: where man and woman are "co-creators, in harmony within hierarchy." Not above God but under God, and "God blessed it . . . soil and spirit are united, heaven and earth are one, there isn't somewhere else . . . the action is here." This condition of paradise is at its core a form of shalom—peace, order, and goodness rule creation, and perfect harmony exists between God and humanity.

However, Bell notes that if one starts the story with Genesis 3, the fall of humankind, the whole tenor of one's ministry, including preaching, shifts dramatically. If one begins with the fall, the emphasis tends to be on sin and salvation; the purpose of Jesus is his death, in order to pay for sin and to open the doors of heaven to sinners. By focusing on this kind of disorder, the shape of the story of salvation moves toward evacuation of the earth and the need to escape to heaven. Bell believes that in the story of the Bible *shalom* bookends history, the beginning and the end—God's creation is revealed in the beginning, and the new creation is consummated in the book of Revelation. As Bell proclaims, "The sermon brings hope, then, hope rooted not in escape but engagement, not in evacuation but reclamation, not in leaving but in staying and overcoming."

Bell marks this as the central theme of the ministry of Jesus Christ: it is "not removal of sin but the restoration of shalom." Shalom is the right ordering of creation so that all, to the glory of God, become co-creators with God in the restoration and reclamation of the world. Of course this reclamation assumes a sinful world rebelling against its maker, fragmented, broken, and alienated from its true nature. Nevertheless, all is not lost, and in Christ the goal of discipleship is to restore the new creation and to proclaim the kingdom of God, the state and condition of shalom.

For Bell, "A sermon then is the continuing insistence that through the resurrection of Jesus a whole new world is bursting forth right here in the midst of this one and everybody and everywhere can be a part of it." The life, death, and resurrection of Jesus Christ inaugurate a new creation, and the church is the extension and messenger of that new story—or as Bell proclaims, "a better story"—that in Christ the world is renewed and humans are remade to reclaim creation and to enjoy the creation as artists, business people, ministers, teachers, social workers, singers, entertainers, and more. The whole world opens itself to the task of sacred reclamation.

But this radical turn that Bell announces over and over again sends chills into some conservative evangelical hearts, causing friction that came to the surface when Bell spoke at his preaching conference in the summer of 2009. Danger stalked Christian conservatives who were close to Rob Bell or using his products. As the preaching conference proceeded, Bell discovered that one of the participants had just been fired for attending a Rob Bell event, despite this pastor having paid his own way and taken his own vacation time to be there.

Long before the *Love Wins* controversy in 2011, Bell had become a marked man in the Reformed evangelical world. In reaction to the pastor's firing and without naming the fired pastor, Bell asked the other attendees if they would contribute financially to sustain the pastor and his family as he looked for other work. After the collection was made, Bell announced that the group had raised $10,000 for the pastor and his family.

A year later, in one of Bell's 2010 sermons, he related the story of the fired pastor. They had become friends. The pastor had been asked by laypeople at his old church to preach, beginning in his backyard at a Sunday picnic. He did so, and soon, 300 people were showing up each Sunday to hear him. In the succeeding Sundays, the crowds became larger and larger. Six months in, the group bought an abandoned opera house, and 10,000 people came through the doors.[16]

In many ways, the story sounds like a way for Bell to stick it in the ear of his critics. But Bell's reaction in the sermon in which he told that story was rather a lament for the young pastor. Echoing words that Bell himself used many times; the young pastor had expressed to Bell, "I'm not a CEO type. I just want to preach." Bell felt the pain of the burden on the young man. Bell's sermon reflected on how aging often makes one "brittle," and how "we get burned, we get criticized, idealism is beaten out of us, we back off, we get a little cynical." It's not hard to see in this Bell's own sense of fatigue, of losing the freshness of the first time and the "greenness" of youth. Bell ended that sermon with a prayer, asking that listeners all be "renewed day by day, and that God would give us a new heart."

Bell had gone through a season of suffering. Returning from Ireland in 2008, a new shift had occurred. His 2009 series on the Sermon on the Mount reflected a man less interested in controlling the outcomes of his work and more invested in the radical nature of Jesus' subversive movement: "Jesus' way threatens the way the world works; the persecuted, theirs is the kingdom . . . God meets you in the poverty of your spirit . . . and announces the ecstatic message that you are my daughter or son. It doesn't start with your success. . . . All healing begins with us admitting our powerlessness." And, without missing a beat, Bell pierces this poignant moment with this

---

16 Rob Bell, "The Village Elder," Mars Hill church, Grandville, MI, August 22, 2010. Sermon. MP3.

sly aside, "Blessed are you when people do evil against you, blog on you, because of me."[17]

Bell accepts that he cannot control what others say or do. He embraces the soul of the artist. He ponders that humans, in their original state before the fall, lived and embodied the way of the artist. In this non-anxious, non-reactive state, "[A]esthetics are there in the beginning; non-efficiency of art reminds us that we are here to enjoy the creation, not to merely use it. Our identity is not based on how hard we work and how much we work. Making things is blessed, and God wants us to enjoy it."[18]

For Bell, the very uselessness of art and art-making parallel the powerlessness and weakness that Jesus blessed in the Sermon on the Mount. Numbers don't matter; nor do converts; nor does labeling something Christian or non-Christian, sacred or secular, clean or unclean; nor do the results of this or that campaign. But rather, it is about making things, beautiful things, co-creating with the Creator, and enjoying it altogether.

The radical nature of this counter-cultural movement could not be more bracing against an American megachurch Christianity that is addicted to results, numbers, budgets, and canned art that "does" or produces something. In contrast, Bell believes that the artist mirrors the Creator, making beauty that is good in itself, to be loved in itself, for itself and not for something else.

This turn bloomed in Bell's sermons after 2008. His 2010 sermon called "The Human Heart is a Mystery" captured this model. This sermon told a rambling summary of the Jonah story and how Jonah disobeyed and "ran away from the Lord." And the sailors, who were pagans and non-Christians, in Bell's words, were actually the ones trying to do the right thing. Bell's summary, filled with asides and stray remarks, confused rather than clarified the story. And yet,

---

17 Rob Bell, "Blessed are the Persecuted," Mars Hill church, Grandville, MI, November 1, 2009. Sermon. MP3.

18 Rob Bell, "Beginning in the Beginning," in *Poets, Prophets & Preachers*, July 2009. Speeches. DVD.

midway, he snapped his listeners to attention, and deadpanned, "The human heart is a mystery."[19]

That's when listeners realized that Bell had made the sermon as incoherent and mysterious as the biblical tale of Jonah. He risked losing his listeners to illustrate the confusing caverns of the human heart. The risk paid off, for there was an anchor in the story, and that anchor was God. "The truth is God will use your obedience or your disobedience. . . . In the midst of the storm, there is one constant, God—making the prophet look silly, petty, petulant, 'If you don't want to go, we'll work with these other guys; it's fine . . . bury your heart, I'll use that too . . . I'm not going to be caught off guard; I made the sea, do you think I can't handle this?'"

At the end of the sermon, Bell turned to Matthew 12:38-42, in which the Pharisees ask Jesus for a sign, and with irony dripping from his every word, Jesus answers, "I give you the sign of Jonah . . . For as Jonah was three days and three nights in the belly of a huge fish, so the Son of Man will be three days and three nights in the heart of the earth." To Bell, this classic rebuke underscores the subversive nature of Jesus' teaching and the artistry of his retort. The sign is not about success but about death and about going against expectation, and through that suffering, finding resurrection. So the way of Jesus is not what is expected—success, winning, control, re- sults—but death and the promise that this descent leads to an ulti- mate victory in resurrection.

Bell's sermon explains that the lesson of Jonah is that despite all of our good intentions, human beings are a mystery—each of us is a mystery to each other and to ourselves. As in Jonah, we don't know why Jonah goes the other way; we don't know why we go the wrong way. We may want to control and manipulate others, but in the end, all go as they will go—we don't have control. Our destiny is not in our hands; it's in God's hands: "God's got it handled, don't be so

---

19 Rob Bell, "The Human Heart is a Mystery," Mars Hill Bible Church, Grandville, MI, February 28, 2010. Sermon. MP3.

judgmental, don't try to control people, God can handle whatever comes God's way." Bell took the risk as a strategic gamble that the listener would stay with him. As the rhetoric mimics the incoherence and mystery of the Jonah story, it snaps into focus by the end. For Bell, this powerful and subversive message leads to the most profound climax in the resurrection, and through it new creation pours forth and reclaims that the earth is the Lord's and everything in it. Bell understands the promise of the reconciliation of all things as the mystery that undergirds his hope, his preaching, and his life.

After Religion

In the fall of 2010 Bell matched his wits with the first vision of the prophet Ezekiel. Ezekiel's visions have been interpreted and reinterpreted over the millennia—by the rabbinic tradition, within the Jewish Kabbalah, by Maimonides, and more recently within the Hasidic traditions. The meaning of the vision varies with each author and tradition. The vision itself is a florid display of poetic imagination that Bell reads with a kind of flourish that brings the piece alive as though the vision might have happened in the very moment of his reading.

In exile during the sixth century BCE, Ezekiel falls down at the edge of the Kabar River in Babylon. His wife is dead, he has lost his homeland, and he is no longer a priest in the temple. Seven hundred miles from his home, God shows up. Ezekiel's first vision itself is extraordinary. God advances on Ezekiel as a divine warrior, rising above him in a battle chariot. Four living creatures each having four faces (of a man, a lion, an ox, and an eagle), and four wings, lead the chariot. Each creature is a wheel within a wheel, and rims are "full of eyes all around," and these "rims are high and awesome."[20]

---

20 Rob Bell, "The Pain is our Teacher," Mars Hill Bible Church, Grandville, MI, September 19, 2010. Sermon. MP3.

Bell, whose artistry mixes with a kind of Barnum and Bailey showmanship, presents Ezekiel through a YouTube video of a monster car with rims that are "high and awesome," and the engines rev. The congregation, who is listening and watching, lets out a squeal. Bell pours points of irony and comedic asides into his presentations. In most of his sermons, just when the scripture or sermon heads toward a kind of solemn climax, Bell pulls back and injects a humorous remark and then, without hesitation, goes right back into his discourse. For some the course change is irreverent, but others find it the key to being drawn in, as humor is juxtaposed against weighty moments of reflection that create a variegated tempo.

In this sermon Bell generates the mood of Ezekiel, who had grown accustomed to but had lost the stability of rules and roles: "Ezekiel is a priest, who facilitates the work of the temple to help people, from all over the world, to make sacrifice, to make peace with their God, the God of Israel." The man is *not* expecting God to make an appearance; the prophet is *not* in the temple; God's presence is *not* in Babylon; the promises of God are *not* for the Babylonians. As Bell nearly yells, "This is Ishtar's House, and it is through the Gate of Ishtar that the captives have been brought." And yet, the vision comes, and the Lord God announces his presence to Ezekiel.

The question for Bell and for Mars Hill, then, is, "What is this all about?" Bell lays down his premise: "Sometimes God goes around the mind, and uses the imagination to get to us to speak directly to our heart. It blows his mind, but it speaks to his heart. It is a personal encounter; a magnificent vision of a kind of monster that has an explosive creativity, and it says, 'I'm here.' Sometimes God has to go directly to your heart."[21]

He then shifts to a story in the New Testament, when the disciples ask Jesus, "Why do you speak to us in parables?" And again, Bell explains, "Parables have a way of going around the mind and speaking directly to the heart." To Bell, the human heart and spirit

---

21 Interview with Rob Bell by author, November 17, 2011.

respond to the story at multiple levels, and experience is not just a rational cost-benefit equation—the human being is a mystery. So to speak to the human spirit takes more than a rational thought or logical equation. Bell's preaching is after that poetic turn and soulful transformation.

More than this, Bell knows the kind of suffering Ezekiel has experienced. His own sense of desolation, his family's trials, the tribulations of so many with whom he has been in ministry—those moments of alienation, joblessness, divorce, abuse, death, and confusion are not easily mitigated by a rational word. But sometimes, as Bell describes, "For many of us our mind is our god. I'm [Bell is talking for God here] going to go around your mind and I'm going to give it to your heart, comfort, grace, because if I give it to your mind, you're going to screw it up." The mystery will be missed, the good word, the peace that passes understanding, cannot be given to the mind but only to the heart.

But the meaning of the story to Ezekiel is not the point for this sermon. Bell is going after another theme. While our assumption may be that God is only and was only ever in the temple, the truth is that God now shows up in exile, in places that no one thought were possible. "And what happens in exile? God shows up in Ishtar's house, in blazing, radiant, luminous, explosive glory, and Ezekiel realizes God is just as much by the river in Babylon; this God cannot be localized. Wherever you go this God is."

Bell is after bigger game in this sermon. The very problem of religion is that it separates and creates a center and periphery. It localizes its god to a place and time, and by definition it argues that all other places and times are less sacred, less holy, less valuable, and that people who worship the other gods, in other places or times, don't have our god and are, therefore, less worthy and less valuable. The center and periphery create boundaries and conflict, tension and violence.

Bell brings this home to his own congregation. When religion argues that heaven is where one will find God, it actually diminishes where one is now, and creates, in a sense, envy, homelessness, and a longing that cannot be filled. And here, Bell comes after the basic constructions of religion that he finds not only unhelpful but unbiblical: "For Ezekiel God is that which is after the temple, after Jerusalem, after Israel, after the altar, after his religion; Ezekiel meets the God who's hanging around after Ezekiel's religion has been blown into a thousand pieces. God is that which can survive even your religion being burned to the ground."

And Bell doesn't stop with Ezekiel. Bell is well aware that in his own life, suffering has come and left him desolate and alone and in exile. Conventional words of comfort have not helped. Bell asks, "What happens then? This isn't just about Ezekiel; God is that who is after our words; God is after our theology, after your doctrine, after your view of the Bible, after your view of Christianity, as you understand that. God can survive even that."

Here Bell demonstrates his core confidence in God, whom Bell believes sustains him even in deep doubt and terrible suffering, "There is nothing to tremble over, the divine is that that is left over when everything else has failed you. Obviously, we love words, we uphold doctrine; we obviously read the Bible, and all at the same time, if that were to burn to the ground, God would be still there holding us in a loving embrace."

Bell's embrace of his transcendental and mystical framework is on full display: God is that which is beyond rational constructs; God is beyond human imaginings; God is beyond and transcends all of our conceiving.

The Center is Everywhere

"A sermon, then," as Bell offers "is never surprised when grace, beauty, meaning, order, compassion, and truth and love show up in all sorts of unexpected people and places because it has been God's world, it is God's world, and it always will be God's world." In this way, Bell suggests, God's presence everywhere makes all holy ground. Everything, if one has eyes to see, "hums with reverence." Labels that bear the name Christian become redundancies, because, in Bell's thinking, whatever is true, beautiful, and good is by its very origin created in Christ and through Christ. Thus, the whole world, wherever those qualities of God are found, is sacred.

One of the most important sources for Bell's thinking on these matters is found in the story of Jacob and his dream at Bethel. Jacob dreams of "angels ascending and descending from heaven." For Bell that connection marks his most treasured insight that heaven and earth are forever entangled, that the action of God is here, and the promise in Revelation 21 that at the end of all things God will dwell with God's people. So, Jacob wakes up and sacralizes his resting place, a common rock under his head, with these words, which for Bell peal like a great bell tower, "When Jacob awoke from his sleep, he thought, 'Surely the LORD is in this place, and I was not aware of it.' He was afraid and said, 'How awesome is this place! This is none other than the house of God; this is the gate of heaven'" (Gen 28:16-17).

Bell asserts that faith is "waking up." The center has not "moved," the "center is everywhere." Bell is fond of claiming, "This changes everything." Fear stalks all when we live as if the "action is somewhere else." This sensibility comes in part from the false assumption that "our true home is somewhere else," a common saying among many conservative evangelicals. This sensibility creates an inner tension that where we are is not where we belong. For Bell, there is a gnawing sensation that someone else or somewhere else is where the action is, and, by implication, our lives are diminished because of it.

If the center is everywhere, and humans by their nature are made in the image of God, and are co-creators with this God, then by definition humans are where the action is, and so, by coming home, waking up, opening our eyes, and realizing that the ground we stand on is by its very nature holy ground, then the whole world becomes sacred. We no longer need to go elsewhere to find our peace, joy, or sense of ecstasy. We have come home to the one who never left.

Bell's fundamental vision captures this profound reunion. It also changes how a person might envision loyalty to one's government and to the vast numbers in the world who live on the edge of survival. We now turn to Bell's radical take on his country and the poor of the world—a position he developed in parallel with his growing sense of the kingdom of God and its demands, which not only challenge a person's sense of loyalty to God, but also create claims for love and justice that go beyond a person's family and nation and extend to the entire global human community.

chapter five

RADICAL

*"So when the commander in chief of the most powerful armed forces
humanity has ever seen quotes the prophet Isaiah from the Bible in celebration
of military victory, we must ask, Is this what Isaiah had in mind? A Christian
should get very nervous when the flag and the Bible start holding hands.
This is not a romance we want to encourage."*

Rob Bell and Don Golden, *Jesus Wants to Save Christians*[1]

The romance between God and country is precisely what so many of
Bell's fellow evangelicals believe in and celebrate—the power of the
United States as a "city upon the hill"; witnessing to its faith in freedom, its faith in democracy, and for many, the core axiom that God
animates and exercises his will both politically and, more precisely,
through the power, heroism, and efficacy of the US military.[2] In-

---

1 See Rob Bell's and Don Golden's *Jesus Wants to Save Christians: A Manifesto
for the Church in Exile.* Grand Rapids, MI: Zondervan, 2008, p. 18.

2 The Puritan John Winthrop in his 1630 sermon "A Model of Christian
Charity," upbraided his future Massachusetts Bay colonists that must become a "city
upon a hill." This notion not only was deeply embedded in the Puritan cultural
DNA but also has become one of the bulwarks for American culture across the
history.

deed, for many, Bell's critique of this relationship is exactly the kind of politicization of religion that Bell says he seeks to avoid. More to the point, his usual ability to allow tensions to stand disappear in *Jesus Wants to Save Christians.* The United States stands condemned as an empire, but did Bell go too far? Clearly, for some, he did. But what makes this period of his life so compelling is that in the midst of his "radical" experiment, he realized that he had stepped over a line that damaged his own faith and threatened the peace within his family.

Did Bell go Too Far?

How far would Bell and Mars Hill go in pursuing this radical critique of nation, church, and the people in it? How far would Bell go in undercutting his own self-constructed image as a "hipster" preacher, able to enthrall people with his innovations, wit and comedic touch?

As it turns out, Bell and his family took it very far. In 2007, the Bells sold many of their possessions and moved into a "crack house" of their own—a remodeled condo in inner city Grand Rapids, where they lived for two years. One of Bell's closest associates at Mars Hill, who discouraged the idea yet helped him move into the neighborhood, described the catcalls from the streets on the day they moved in, "What do you want, you white blah, blah, blah." Bell's close friend and lay leader in the church who hated *Jesus Wants to Save Christians* unloaded on Bell, "What are you doing here? You don't fit in here; you just think you do." He said with a sarcastic smile, "You're going to cool your way into this neighborhood?"[3]

Nowhere in Bell's sermons or writings did the fact come to light that he had made this move into the inner city. I heard it inadvertently. Bell told me later that he had spoken about it only once in public, in only direct response to a question from an audience member, "The preacher who's always telling you all the great things he's doing, that's not the right way to do it in my opinion. Quietly, you

---

3 Interview with Rob Bell associate by author, November 19, 2011.

go about working out your own salvation and it involves all sorts of interesting things." Bell's tumble of motivations revealed that this "work" of salvation was hardly clear to him. He made the move in part to avoid the embarrassment that "if they come and do an exposé on me, they're not going to find a mansion." And in part it involved Bell's relentless inquisitiveness: "I'm insatiably curious, so I wanted to live in an area that was not safe, and I want to know, wanted to understand it in a visceral way." The Bells lived with one car. Bell explained, "I walked everywhere."[4]

In the end, living one doorway from the street drained Bell's time and energies. The short distance between the dangerous streets, in which Bell reported numerous shootings, took its toll. And perhaps, most importantly, Bell told me that it affected his faith:

> The gospel of denial can begin to affect you in profound ways, like when you are endlessly cutting yourself off . . . it becomes harder to announce a grace, which is generous and bountiful . . . God's love is a lavish over the top gift. And you actually have this conflict with Jesus and his disciples, because that money could be used for the poor, or it could be a demonstration of a God who lavishes us with love. And I think I've been at different places at different times in my life. Possessions can be a vehicle for your experiences of the divine; they can also be a barrier."[5]

This insatiable desire to investigate the full experience of living in Christ pushed Bell in unexpected ways. Some might wonder whether Bell put his family in danger as he tried to live out this call to solidarity with the oppressed. For Bell, the radical nature of discipleship by biblical standards is something quite different altogether: "Take up their cross and follow me" (Matt 16:24, CEB). But the meaning of this verse for him was far from clear. What did this mean to him personally and for his family? What would it mean for

---

4 Interview with Rob Bell by author, March 1, 2012.
5 Interview with Rob Bell by author, November 19, 2011.

a church to follow this path institutionally? Bell, with his usual impulsiveness, would find out.

The Experiment Begins

In September 2006, Bell had recently returned from a speaking tour (*Everything is Spiritual*) that included 28 events over the course of 30 days. With his energy renewed, he announced that his latest book, *Jesus Wants to Save Christians,* was nearly done. It would be his most controversial book yet—challenging the very of heart of evangelical piety and politics—and taking direct aim at the practices of fellow megachurch ministers.

Once again, the several sides of Rob Bell tumbled and crashed into one another: the slick celebrity wannabe and the emerging Hebrew prophet, calling his people to the "new exodus." During the year before and after the publication of *Jesus Wants to Save Christians,* Bell confronted these multiple versions of himself and the issues that each one brought into question. We have witnessed Bell's subversive side, how he plunged into forms of suffering as ways of knowing God. And we have also seen how this played up against the pop diva Bell, filled with juice, levity, and comic wit that attracted crowds at Mars Hill. But his prophetic side also emerged, questioning the pretensions and ambitions of megachurches, such as the easy collaboration of the conservative evangelical church and the state, including its support for the Iraq war. With this new side emerging, Bell demanded from his church and his readers not only a form of spiritual but also social transformation.

Bell didn't spare anyone in his prophetic critique. On the back cover of *Jesus Wants to Save Christians,* he described how a rich church in Grand Rapids had spent $20 million on itself next to the staggering statistic that 20 percent of Grand Rapid's citizens lived in poverty. This statistic suggests, as his book details, that Christian churches that focus on glorious buildings and ignore social justice miss the very heart of the gospel. Bell's words and rhetoric in this period suggest a zero-sum game; money spent on one thing takes money from another. But Bell seemed unaware of the ramifications of his own heated rhetoric, as if the statements didn't imply judgment.

A part of Bell's attractiveness had been his youthful naiveté—a wit and comic touch that lightened the mood and spliced a sense of humor into the midst of a sober moment. But the other side of that seeming innocence was how the words he spoke casually provoked effects that reverberated throughout his church and into the broader public. It's hard to be a rock star pastor and a prophet all wrapped in one. Bell's fearlessness could, on occasion, slide into a kind of foolishness, a line that he flirted with regularly. How he negotiated these tensions within his religious family takes us deeper into his complex journey.

The Mark of the Beast

Jim Henderson, in his recent book *The Resignation of Eve* argues that although there are numerous exceptions, evangelicals tend to focus on personal sins and either ignore or rationalize systemic or structural sin.[6] Bell's ministry, and particularly *Jesus Wants to Save Christians,* is a full-on confrontation with the systematic politicization of the American evangelical church. Not only do politics and religion make deadly partners, but Bell also compares the American empire to the violent empires of the past, such as the Egyptians who enslaved the Hebrews and the Romans who killed Jesus. "America is an empire . . . what's true of empires then is true of empires now. What we see in the Bible is that empires naturally accumulate wealth and resources."[7] Bell quotes George H. W. Bush on how "the American Lifestyle is not up for negotiation" and goes on to argue that the great temptation of empires is "entitlement," the sense that its privileges are not only earned but also deserved. As Bell slyly meditates,

---

6 Henderson's distinction on the prioritization of the personal over the social was confirmed in my research on twenty-four evangelical churches in *Evangelical vs. Liberal: The Clash of Christians Cultures in the Pacific Northwest*. NY: Oxford University Press, 2008.

7 Rob Bell and Don Golden, *Jesus Wants to Save Christians*, p. 121.

"Imagine hearing this as one of the three billion people on the planet who survive on two dollars a day."[8]

Bell's central thesis is that while winners may write history, "God always hears the cry of the oppressed."[9] This proposition, while powerful as far as it goes, remains debatable. Does God always hear the cry of the oppressed? Many of those in the Jewish tradition have debated this notion. After the Holocaust, many Jews denied God's very existence because, in their eyes, God did not act. Their prayers went unanswered. For Christians, Jesus is often designated as *the* answer to the cry of oppressed—to the "sin-sick" in evangelical circles—but to what end? Does Jesus save the soul and leave one in poverty? Does conversion mean prosperity and the chance to be successful? Success, or its promise, dominates in many evangelical traditions—and in the megachurch movement, in particular.

Moreover, conservative American Christians tend to interpret American hegemony in the world as God-granted and God-ordained. Faithfulness produces American prosperity and is good not only for America but also for the world. But this isn't just a conservative Christian tendency; there is a long tradition in both liberal and more conservative American Christian religious traditions of the belief that American strength is good for the globe.[10]

Nevertheless, in *Jesus Wants to Save Christians,* Bell doesn't equivocate. God hears the oppressed and answers. God expects the blessed not only to hear the oppressed but to be in solidarity with them. A nation's success is only as good as its ability to share and care for those who are left out and left behind. The problem is that empires, more often than not, become entitled. And at the heart of entitlement is the notion that a country is special, exceptional. Bell questions the proposition that a nation's blessings are deserved and

---

8 Rob Bell and Don Golden, *Jesus Wants to Save Christians*, p. 125.

9 Rob Bell and Don Golden, *Jesus Wants to Save Christians*, p. 53.

10 See my article with S.R. Thompson "From the Social Gospel to Neoconservativism: Religion and U.S. Foreign Policy."

should be preserved. And by doing so, Bell calls into question the very nature of America's soul.

But Bell goes even further by contending that in the book of Revelation the "mark of the Beast" is the "way humans misuse power to accumulate and stockpile while others suffer and starve."[11] Bell questions the very possibility that a powerful nation can resist the temptation of entitlement and resist becoming another Egypt, another Babylon, or even another Rome.

Bell gave a sermon on the Iraq War. He argued that the plan for war was flawed, motivated by the American need for energy resources and security. The sermon did not remain on the Mars Hill's website. "Maybe they took it down," Bell explained. "We lost a lot of people after that one; there were parents with kids in the Iraq War."[12] Bell held nothing back, challenging the motivation of America's place in the world and the unjust nature of the Iraq invasion as a preemptive war.

More to the point, Bell asked difficult questions about how churches should live and act in the midst of empires. Do they continue to build extensions to their buildings? Do they hire additional staff who serve the "needs" of their "consumers"? Do they emphasize theologies that are purely individualistic, focusing first and foremost on personal salvation? Do ministries target personal sins alone, aiming, for instance, at whether young people are having or have had pre-marital sex? Do churches become cheerleaders for their national empires? Do they baptize national greed and create theologies that ordain militaries and support violence as forms of redemptive violence?

Bell asserts that Jesus *literally* wants to save Christians from this type of constriction and collusion. The idea is that these forms of privatized Christianity thrive on insulating the church from the needs of the world. Their theologies allow the church to ignore the deprivation of much of the world because God cares first and foremost about souls. There is little doubt that this line of thought tends

---

11 Rob Bell and Don Golden, *Jesus Wants to Save Christians*, p. 133.
12 Interview with Rob Bell by author, March 1, 2012.

to skew and stereotype evangelicals when we know that there is a growing sensitivity to these kinds of political entanglements and the danger to the people they serve. Moreover, international missionaries often are at the heart of justice advocacy—this is true in particular in relation to evangelicals coming out of Europe.[13] At the same time, churches and missionaries in this context, often without intending to be, become chaplains for the state, ordaining forms of state corruption and violence.[14]

Bell's critique of this kind of theological system that ignores injustice and sustains nation-states is what he calls an "anti-kingdom"; it overlooks human misery and ignores systems that cement social inequality and brutalize the enemies of the empire. Here, the radical nature of Bell's frontal assault on the Christian church could not be any clearer. For Bell, if Jesus gets angry, it's not because teenagers have had premarital sex. It's because a billion people in the world lack access to adequate water while churches don't lift a finger to help. This is unacceptable to Bell. Any system that allows this kind of misery, whether Christian or otherwise, carries the mark of the Beast.

Bell threw down the gauntlet, and some evangelicals scrambled to throw it right back.

"I hated that book," exclaimed one of Bell's closest friends and a lay leader at Mars Hill, who noted that he shared that sentiment with Bell. The lay leader explained, "That was part of the Don Golden era. God is green; Jesus wants to save Christians, the neo-cons and all that." For Bell's friend, the exercise amounted to a "waste of time," proving to many that "Rob's an ass." The friend told me with a smile that he and Bell participated in many "tough exchanges over

---

13 See Matthew Keyes and the author, "Portable Politics and Durable Religion: The Moral Worldviews of American Evangelical Missionaries. *Sociology of Religion* 2007, 68:4, pp. 383-406.

14 See Clark Lombardi's and my edited volume on *Religion and Human Security: A Global Perspective.* NY: Oxford University Press, 2012. There are several chapters detailing the political complexities that evangelicals face overseas, particularly in African nations.

politics,"[15] but that each walked away with mutual admiration. Bell didn't back down.

Don Golden, Bell's co-author on *Jesus Wants to Save Christians*, was a "lead pastor" at Mars Hill from 2005 to 2008. Golden, with a background with World Relief—a global non-profit relief agency, sought to bring greater efficiency and responsiveness to the large global outreach at Mars Hill. The administrative side of Golden's work received mixed reviews. Nonetheless, Bell embraced Golden's partnership to offer a prophetic critique of the American evangelical church and the American empire.

Another of Bell's lay leaders who also rejected the book described her deep appreciation for Bell's work and his willingness to take risks, reminding us that a prophet is not often welcome in their own house, even as they "prod us to look critically at every theology, examining it in light of the example of Jesus."[16] Both of the lay leaders who challenged Bell's and Golden's analyses expressed enormous regard for Bell, even though they differed with Bell in their political affiliations.

Bell's commitment to solidarity with the poor translated into what he didn't do—he forewent interest in enlarging or remodeling the Mars Hill church building. He created a philosophy of ministry that argued that the real ministry of Mars Hill happened outside its walls, in places of great need. And Bell did not stress over losing Mars Hill attendees, whether the thousand who left following his preaching in favor of women in ministry, or those who left after his case against the Iraq War. This was part of Bell's preternatural confidence that new people would just keep coming, as well as his fearlessness that consistently came across in interviews with Bell explaining, "What do I have to lose?" Indeed, early on, when a group of Mars Hill members sought (unsuccessfully) to revoke his ordination in response to his movement to include women in leadership (and with implications regarding his interpretation of scripture), he laughed, "Oh, what would I do without those papers?"

---

15 Interview with Rob Bell associate by author, November 19, 2011.
16 Interview with Rob Bell associate by author, November 18, 2011.

At the same time, Bell intentionally stayed close to church leaders who ferociously disagreed with him. Bell combined a ruthless critique of political systems with a light touch. He valued the integrity of individuals who took different perspectives, and he didn't waver in his respect and friendship. Whether this was a matter of convenience, equanimity, or his own doubts about his prophetic critique, it marked him as someone willing to take risks and hold positions in some tension—a tension that began to take a toll.

More Important Matters

This very independence spurred Bell's desire to push his own thinking and theology in new directions, to challenge himself and his congregation as well. To some extent, Bell's sense of humor and his ability to stay flexible smoothed and mitigated the hard edges of what he expressed in *Jesus Wants to Save Christians*. Nonetheless, he laid down an agenda for the congregation and continued to challenge the essential priorities of his own congregation's evangelical culture.

In the fall of 2007, Bell's sermon "Gnats and Camels" argued that obedience to religious laws often obscures the "more important" principles of faith. In his prototypical manner, he interrogated the Matthew 23:23 text: "Woe to you, teachers of the law and Pharisees, you hypocrites! You give a tenth of your spices—mint, dill and cumin. But you have neglected the more important matters of the law—justice, mercy and faithfulness. You should have practiced the latter, without neglecting the former." Bell continued:

> The Pharisees, in their attempt to win God's favor had missed the more important central agenda of God's justice, mercy, and faithfulness . . . You have neglected the suffering of the world. God's heart beats for the suffering of the world. Some people say, it's all about me and God; when it all comes down to it, it's just about me and God. It sounds great, but it's not what Jesus teaches. Personal holiness is important . . . it's not that you should neglect this, but it makes some people miss the central things: justice, compassion, and mercy. . . .

God isn't just interested in saving you, and God is not just interested in you and your purity. God wants to use us to do something about the greatest suffering in the world.

In dozens of Bell's sermons, personal holiness in thought, word, and deed was held up as important. He did not neglect this aspect of the faith. For him, there was no either/or. A person's faith necessitates serious moral examination. Personal and political allegiances and actions were to be continually weighed and considered.

Indeed, for Bell, the biblical moral universe is prophetic at its core: "What is unique to the biblical narrative is self-critique. . . ." In Bell's mind, the biblical narrative is constantly questioning its own assumptions. It is willing to argue with God and it challenges the righteousness of Israel. It claims that God is present everywhere and not only in the temple. It entirely upends its own expectations about the Messiah, and it pours grace to the Gentile.

Bell believes the interrogative mode is the biblical interpretive key, "As a Christian, a person of faith then, critique of yourself, church, community, nation is central to a vibrant life in the world. And a discussion about spending ten billion dollars a month on a war should be as basic as breathing. This should not even be remotely controversial."[17]

The prophetic imagination spares no area of the moral and spiritual life, either personal or political. And Bell put his own positions under the same moral microscope. While Bell held his moral and religious positions with a sense of confidence, he drew out the radical implications for himself, as we have seen, but also for Mars Hill.

God Needs a Body

Bell argued that from the covenant given on Mt. Sinai, God called his people to be "a kingdom of priests and a holy nation." The priests mediate the relationship between God and humankind, and Bell

---

17 Interview with Rob Bell by author, March 1, 2012.

insists that these priests, like so many other Biblical stories and characters, are "an invitation to show the world who this God is and what this God is like."[18] They become his body. And what is Bell's God like? He is a God who speaks truth to power, a God who cares for the "orphan and the widow," a God that led the slaves from Egypt, and a God who confronts God's people when, in their strength, they forget the weak, the stranger, the orphan, the widow, and the foreigner. This is what Bell's God is like.

Bell illustrates God's awareness that God's people fall and fail: "And now Solomon is building a temple to the God who sets slaves free . . . using slaves?"[19] The prophetic imagination relentlessly confronts those who become strong and then take advantage and feel entitled: "Jerusalem is the new Egypt. Solomon is the new Pharaoh."[20] The Bible, as Bell points out, shows how the prophets repeatedly remind the people of where they came from and that God is the God of the oppressed and this God hears the "blood cry out . . . from the ground." Bell argues that this cry haunts the scriptures but also knows it is a cry too often ignored. God needs a body who will listen.

In Bell's June 2007 sermon, he asked "Do you realize how far we are taking this?" He laid out his agenda for Mars Hill: "I want to talk to you about what it means to be fully human. I want to talk to you about implications of what we're doing here."[21] Moving quickly and effectively through several gospel passages, Bell landed on John 14, where Jesus promises that "whoever believes in me will do the works I have been doing, and they will do even greater things than these" (John 14:12). Bell rouses his congregation, telling them Jesus' followers are like these mighty companions. "Be careful if you follow Jesus, Jesus has a high view of humanity; people are capable of greatness."

---

18 Rob Bell and Don Golden, *Jesus Wants to Save Christians*, p. 31.

19 Rob Bell and Don Golden, *Jesus Wants to Save Christians*, p. 39.

20 Rob Bell and Don Golden, *Jesus Wants to Save Christians*, p. 43.

21 Rob Bell, "Do you realize how far we are taking this?" Mars Hill Bible Church, Grandville, MI, June 3, 2007. Sermon. MP3.

For Bell, however, this greatness is neither about a Christian nationalism nor an upbeat prosperity gospel. Jesus' followers redeem the world through the work of peace and justice. At the beginning of 2007, in a set of sermons two weeks apart, Bell had two members of Mars Hill tell their stories. One is the story of Rachel, a young woman who had recently graduated from Calvin College. Trained to be a teacher, she applied to work in an alternative school in the inner city of Grand Rapids, rather than the more typical suburban school. Rachel told a story of endemic violence, broken families, and the murder of one of her students. Gangs, drugs, and family violence shape the very fabric of these kids' lives, but Rachel maintained a compassionate detachment: "Some people ask me if I feel any fear or danger in that school, and its true I feel that way at times, but more dangerous if I had built walls around me so I couldn't hear the cries of the oppressed: living a life of complacency. To be living with them is not only for them but for us. God writes the story of the Bible because we are supposed to be in that story. Some people believe but don't join in the story."[22]

Bell's listeners internalized his prophetic vision in ways that one might imagine shocked and disturbed others, like the parents of this Calvin College graduate. Rachel, in her story, pricks the conscience of the Mars Hill congregation, declaring, "Yes, we need money . . . not to quell our conscience with a check, but we need to be with the poor to recognize their faces, to see them not as an 'other,' but to feel what they feel."

And this voice of solidarity with the poor, God's body in action for the oppressed, took root in the hearts and minds of some of the 40,000 or so weekly podcast listeners across the globe. Six months after Rachel spoke to the Mars Hill congregation, Bell narrated how Rachel had moved on from her Grand Rapids alternative high school to start teaching at an even more dangerous school in Denver, a school for street kids. Bell quipped, tongue in cheek, "Yes, Jesus is

---

22 Rob Bell, "The School by the Side of the Road," Mars Hill Bible Church, Grandville, MI, June 3, 2007. Sermon. MP3.

all about the path of ascent." He explained how Rachel met a fellow teacher who had been a Marine, who had gone to seminary, and then signed up for the same Denver school. Rachel asked him what he was doing there, and he explained, "'Well, I listen to a weekly podcast from a church in Grand Rapids. Earlier this year, Rob interviewed this young woman, and I heard her story, and I knew I had to give my life to the kids everybody else has forgotten." Rachel looked at him, "I am that woman."[23]

Two weeks after telling this first story about Rachel, Bell interviewed another Mars Hill attendee named Marilyn. She tells of how she and her husband, a minister himself, had moved with their three young children into a Grand Rapids inner city "former crack house."

Marilyn, with joy and wit, describes how their mission was simply to be a "presence for Jesus Christ" in the neighborhood. Mars Hill remodeled the home, and provided the startup costs. Marilyn and her husband did odd jobs and began to "minister" by taking walks on their block. Children from the neighborhood started following them and became friends with Marilyn's young kids. They visited her home. They initiated a tutoring program and clothing drive for the children in the area, and slowly but surely the neighborhood began to change.

A police officer, who several years earlier searched for drugs in the house that Marilyn and her family had moved into, also became involved in the ministry. After some time, the police officer and his family (somewhat reluctantly) moved into the neighborhood. The tutoring programs expanded, and childcare programs grew dramatically as more and more Mars Hill attenders got involved and gave money.

The purpose of what Marilyn and her family felt resonated in her voice and attitude. Bell picked up on this and summarized the powerful motivation that was a gift given but also a gift received from the people to whom Marilyn and her family ministered: "So, your relationship with God is so powerful that you can't imagine doing any other thing, it just flows from who you are . . . you can't

---

23 Rob Bell, "Gnats and Camels," Mars Hill Bible Church, Grandville, MI, September 30, 2007. Sermon. MP3.

imagine being any other way . . . So, fearless, courageous living is the most normal way imaginable."[24]

Bell and Mars Hill listened. Then Bell probed, "What if the church converted to Jesus? . . . What if instead of the church *having* a mission, what if the church *was* the mission—its very organizational heart served the poor, helped the needy, and listened to the cry of the oppressed? . . . If you had a couple thousand priests in one place, the earth would tremble."[25]

Bell then took the notion of the priesthood of all believers and challenged the church to become a radical tribe of caregivers—God's ministerial body in the world. This goes to the heart of the way he questions the role of missionaries. Bell believes that setting some aside as "missionaries" undercuts the notion that everyone in the church is in mission. To call some missionaries sends all the wrong messages—that somehow business people, educators, or social workers are not missionaries. Everyone, if they are a Christian, is in full-time ministry. For Bell, the idea that churches should be sending money to separate organizations that feed the poor or help the needy makes little sense. Why isn't the church doing this social service? Or as he would say, "Why do the agencies get to have all the fun?"

Can a Church be Converted?

Bell tried to live what he preached. It didn't work for him and his family, or at least it didn't work in the ways he thought it should. Nonetheless, he kick-started this radical gospel at Mars Hill. Don Golden partnered with Bell in these efforts, but Golden himself had his own doubts, which Bell narrated in a sermon in the middle of 2007. He summarized a conversation that Golden had participated in with a global expert on poverty: "Don asked this guy, 'Can the church be converted to the great causes of the day?' The guy said, 'The big suburban churches, no, it can't be done. If you really want

---

24 Rob Bell, "The Most Normal Thing Imaginable," Mars Hill Bible Church, Grandville, MI, June 21, 2007. Sermon. MP3.

25 Rob Bell, "Do you realize how far we are taking this?"

to see the kingdom expand, you go over to this agency [independent non-profit relief organizations] to make an impact. The church, no, those people only think about themselves. They might write a check sometimes.'"[26]

Bell gave this illustration and then reminded Mars Hill of the vision Golden had laid out for Mars Hill: "Let's be crystal clear on Don's vision for us—a profound vision that Don has given our church—the biblical example is urban renewal, poverty alleviation, the Church is the mission." What's fascinating here is that Bell proclaims "Don's vision for the Mars Hill church." Was it Bell's vision? And perhaps more to the point was it Mars Hill's vision? Whatever doubts Bell had about this vision, he gave it a great effort. He lived with his family in an inner-city condo for two years; he pared back his own personal possessions, and Mars Hill stepped up.

In 2001, Mars Hill partnered with World Relief to give one million dollars over seven years to rescue Africans from AIDS. In 2007, under Don Golden's leadership, Mars Hill was awarded a grant of nearly ten million from the George W. Bush administration to further AIDS education in several African nations. Mars Hill also made a large push for the water filter mechanism that its members had created for communities in various parts of Africa. More generally, the congregation gave approximately 25 percent of its annual six million dollar budget in mission—an impressive record relative to nearly any church in the nation.

But the uphill task of personal and social transformation for his life, family, and church created a cul-de-sac from which Bell had to escape. In the spring of 2008, Bell told his leadership that he needed to take time off. That was the summer he went to Ireland.

This was the beginning of the end of Bell's ministry at Mars Hill. How far could a pastor take a church? How far could a person push a church to reflect a radical and prophetic ministry of solidarity with the oppressed, the poor, and the marginalized? As far as Bell

---

26 Rob Bell, "Do you realize how far we are taking this?"

took it, he still ran up against his own personal limitations, and the limits of a local church. Was Bell on the fine line between foolishness and fearlessness? Was it foolish to expect a diverse congregation, coming from a conservative region of the country, to buy into a radical gospel that challenged core principles of the conservative American middle class?

Bell had questioned whether preemptive war against Iraq was moral and ethical. He probed whether America's sense of privilege and entitlement was either deserved or noble. He interrogated Americans' tendency toward wealth and entitlement. He asked whether living in safety rather than in solidarity with the oppressed was even moral. He challenged whether a congregation should even have missionaries, per se. He contested the whole notion that a church should partner with non-profits and relief agencies. His radical questions threatened the taken-for-granted conventions not only of evangelical life but also of even more powerful middle-class American life.

Did Bell go too far? Does the gospel go too far? His own passion and desire to change the church drove him finally toward a sense of his own powerlessness, a sense that he couldn't control this or any church. No church or community was going to really change the inner city, and no minister could reinvent the church.

Did Bell Go Far Enough?

In the fall of 2009 and the winter of 2010, Bell gave a set of teachings on the Beatitudes from the Sermon on the Mount. Earlier in this book, we looked at those sermons exploring how even in the depths of our sorrow and poverty of spirit, God blesses each person. In a sermon in January 2010, Bell taught on Jesus' command, "Do not judge" (Matt 7:1). And he declared "When we judge and criticize others, we fail to entrust others to God . . . if you don't entrust others to God, you will be plagued by judgment of others; judgment rooted in our desire to control." Perhaps Bell was reflecting on his own relationship to Mars Hill. He couldn't control them, and in the end had to let them be who they were, just as he had to be himself.

To Bell this acknowledgement didn't suggest that his estimation of the American empire or his critique of American entitlement were wrong. Neither did he reject his passionate belief in the priesthood of all believers. In fact, he would later plead, "Ordain everyone. Call everyone a minister; invite the whole church to be on staff."[27] Bell continued to believe that radical service and care of creation is the way of the gospel. And his passion in seeking to spread this message remained intact. He took his perspective and asked powerful questions about the country, the church, and the very heart of what it means to be a follower of Jesus.

When prodded on why he pushed things to the limit, Bell reflected with a sense of pathos: "You become broken enough, fear is no longer interesting, or compelling, you then become like electric . . . because you don't fear anymore . . . really, you're going to criticize me . . . but do you really think this is going to slow me down? Like, its already happened, already had my best friend betray me. It's all happened; it's all already happened and we're still here."[28]

In 2009, the pendulum of the radical and prophetic activist seemed to swing back in the other direction, from social revolutionary to the safer and less disruptive rostrum of personal transformation. Bell's ministry, while energized following his sojourn to Ireland, seemed to move away from his prophetic critique of the Don Golden years. If there was passion, it was about the personal journey of creativity and self-discovery. This manifested itself both in the book *Love Wins* and also in his preaching, which dealt with issues of self-transcendence and self-discovery in God. In an interview in 2012, following his stepping down from Mars Hill, Bell pitched a vision that mined this area of personal transformation and the kingdom of God:

> We have to embrace our desires. For many, desire is a bad word, something we're supposed to 'give up for God.' That

27 Skye Jethani, "Hello, Rob Bell – The Interview." *Huffington Post, Religion:* The Blog, March 1, 2012. http://www.huffingtonpost.com/skye-jethani/hello-rob-bell_b_1307329.html. Accessed March 4, 2012.

28 Interview with Rob Bell by author, March 1, 2012.

kind of thinking can be really destructive because it teaches people to deny their hearts, their true selves. What Jesus does is something far more radical. He insists that we can be transformed in such a way that our desires and God's desires for us become the same thing. Incredible. What do you love to do that brings more and more heaven into God's good world? What is it that makes your soul soar? What is it that you do, that your friends and community affirm, that taps you in to who you are made to be?[29]

In this post-Mars Hill interview, Bell is no longer speaking about the church as mission, but is focusing on individuals who create from a soul-centered passion for the true self.

This is a far throw from the radical theology of liberation and solidarity. Toward the end of *Jesus Wants to Save Christians*, Bell makes two statements, the first, in tune with his call for social transformation, "Jesus wants to save us from preaching a gospel that is only about individuals and not about the systems that enslave them."[30] In the second statement, an inkling of the more recent Bell, the one who penned *Love Wins*, comes to the fore: "Jesus wants to save us from shrinking the gospel down to a transaction about the removal of sin and not about every single particle of creation being reconciled to its maker."[31]

This later Bell resonates most powerfully in his last years at Mars Hill. And it's the Bell whom we discover in *Love Wins*, the Bell we will meet in the following chapter. What's perhaps most surprising is that much of the material shaping *Love Wins* is drawn from subjects that were implicit in Bell's earlier preaching at Mars Hill. In that sense, *Love Wins* was more predictable and certainly less provocative than the Bell we met in *Jesus Wants to Save Christians*. Nevertheless, the controversy of *Love Wins* made the book a bestseller and catapulted Bell to new heights; it also got him labeled as a heretic by some.

---

29 Skye Jethani, "Hello, Rob Bell—The Interview."
30 Rob Bell and Don Golden, *Jesus Wants to Save Christians*, p. 179.
31 Rob Bell and Don Golden, *Jesus Wants to Save Christians*, p. 179.

The *Love Wins* hullabaloo, perhaps unexpectedly, became Bell's bon voyage out of the Reformed evangelical world. This journey, and its many bumps and bruises, created the drama explored in the next chapter. The irony of it all is that it's not the radical prophetic critique that ejected him from the evangelical camp, but questions about heaven and hell—which may say more about the Reformed evangelical world than it does about Bell.

chapter six

HERETIC

"At the very heart of this controversy, and one of the reasons the blogosphere exploded over this book, is that we really do have two different Gods. The stakes are that high. If Bell is right, then historic orthodoxy is toxic and terrible. But if the traditional view of heaven and hell are right, Bell is blaspheming. I do not use the word lightly, just like Bell probably chose 'toxic' quite deliberately. Both sides cannot be right. As much as some voices in evangelicalism will suggest that we should all get along and learn from each other and listen for the Spirit speaking in our midst, the fact is we have two irreconcilable views of God."

Kevin DeYoung, "A Review of *Love Wins* by Rob Bell"[1]

The publication of *Love Wins* in March 2011 created an avalanche of controversy and publicity for Bell and his book. John Piper, the leader to the neo-Reformed movement, tweeted, "Farewell Rob Bell." Others, like Justin Taylor (a blogger and a keeper of the neo-Reformed movement), without even having read the book, proclaimed, "It is unspeakably sad when those called to be ministers of the Word

---

1 See Kevin DeYoung's "God is Still Holy and what you learned in Sunday school is Still True: A Review of *Love Wins* by Rob Bell."

distort the gospel and deceive the people of God with false doctrine."[2] Taylor, later on in the same blog entry, linked to Kevin DeYoung's review of *Love Wins,* in which DeYoung accused Bell of "damaging human souls." Bell's detractors were quick to answer with books of their own. The popular evangelical writer (and former megachurch pastor) Francis Chan penned *erasing hell: what God said about eternity, and the things we've made up*; Mark Galli, a senior managing editor for *Christianity Today,* charged into the conversation with *God Wins: Heaven, Hell, and Why the Good News is Better than Love Wins.* Others books followed, but Chan and Galli led the attack. While Chan claimed to be Bell's "friend", both Galli and Chan argued that their books weren't even about *Love Wins.*[3]

With *Love Wins,* Bell held nothing back. He went public with his thinking about heaven and hell even as he had been preaching and working through many of the ideas in various forums previously, but the book's publication brought his unconventional beliefs to a much broader audience. Tony Jones' comments on the aftermath hit the target: "[Bell]'s gone rogue. *Rob Bell is the Jason Bourne of Christianity.* Meanwhile, Piper and the rest of his tribe have been waiting to pounce on Rob Bell. I've been saying in private for several years that the Evangelical Intelligentsia is looking for a reason to turn on Rob. This is their chance. Rob is big and influential and, since they don't agree with his theology, they want to turn him out. They want their followers to stop buying his books."[4]

Evangelicals, at least many in the conservative and neo-Reformed side of Protestantism, ejected Bell from the "acceptable and lauded" group of evangelical luminaries. But what was it in *Love Wins* that created these scorching responses? Theologically, how did

---

2 See Justin Taylor's blog post "Rob Bell: Universalist?" on The Gospel Coalition website, February 26, 2011. http://thegospelcoalition.org/blogs/justin taylor/2011/02/26/rob-bell-universalist/. Accessed March 1, 2012.

3 See Francis Chan's and Preston Sprinkle's *erasing hell.* See also Mark Galli's *God Wins: Heaven, Hell, and Why the Good News is Better than Love Wins.* Carol Stream, IL: Tyndale House Publishers, Inc. 2011.

4 See Tony Jones' blog, "What's Up With Rob Bell?" Author italics.

Bell step out of the bounds of a putative evangelical Christian orthodoxy? And how, for many evangelicals, did Bell transgress the conventional terms of Christian soteriology—the terms and conditions of Christian salvation? But an even more explosive charge came to the forefront: is Rob Bell a heretic?

Home Cooking

Much of the material from *Love Wins* emerged from Bell's talks and sermons at Mars Hill. Nonetheless, those around him knew, certainly better than Bell, that with the publication of *Love Wins* there would be hell to pay. In fact, one of Bell's associates admitted, "The *Love Wins* thing really shocked him. I read the manuscript, and went, 'Oh shit.' I told him, 'Dude, this is not going to go well,'" but Bell remained almost blasé about it. To this associate and countless others, his response was invariably this: "It's just for conversation." But the friend was right—Bell's gift for creative expression and audacious questions (350 of them in *Love Wins*) met with mixed reviews. Bell's friend explained that Bell approaches "complex issues with a childlike wonder." But not everyone appreciates Bell's childlike curiosity. [5]

And yet, across the board, from those I interviewed at Mars Hill, the reaction to Bell's theological provocations created a sense of relief. Bell's congregation had permission to ask questions they assumed forbidden: "Oh, are we allowed to do that?"—"Yes!"

Bell did not fear that his congregation couldn't stomach tough questions, or that they would be "corrupted." A significant number of members, however, left Mars Hill following the book's publication. But for those who stayed, *Love Wins* extended this Bellian form of teaching. As another lay associate explained, "It's more of an eastern mindset. Don't be afraid to look at the object from all different sides. It's OK. Don't be afraid to walk out of there more confused than when you walked in. It's OK. But in a traditional church

---

5 Interview with Rob Bell associate by author, November 19, 2011.

setting, it's horrifying, because what you're saying is the emperor has no clothes."[6]

Bell trusted that his congregation would think for themselves, and that *Love Wins* was but one way of approaching complex ideas. He believed that he was broadcasting the thoughts and questions that everyone was thinking but that few, particularly within the evangelical community, dared even whisper.

At the same time, in subtle and not so subtle ways, Bell threw down the gauntlet. In an interview between Mark Galli and Francis Chan, Galli commented on the sting of Bell's seemingly innocent thoughts, "I think that's where Rob is a little disingenuous. He claims he's not a controversialist, but when it comes to his critique of fundamentalist and legalistic Christianity, he spares no sarcasm." Chan responded, "That was the hard part for me. I didn't see love toward those people—among whom I would be included. In some of those respects it seemed like a mockery of what I believe and the God that I believe in." [7] True to form, in Bell's sermons the legalists received a major broadside.

In his sermon "Converts to Hell," Bell laid down a torrid critique of traditional evangelism. Taking his cue from the Matthew 23:15 text, he read: "Woe to you, teachers of the law and Pharisees, you hypocrites! You travel over land and sea to win a single convert, and when you have succeeded, you make them twice as much a child of hell as you are." He began to ask questions, "How did Jesus talk about faith, witness to his faith? How did he compel people and not do it in a destructive way?"[8]

Bell considered how Jesus deploys various metaphors to explain what faith is like. Jesus didn't use heavy-handed formulas of belief or

---

6 Interview with Rob Bell associate by author, November 19, 2011.

7 Mark Galli, "Q&A: Francis Chan on Rob Bell and Hell," *Christianity Today Magazine,* July 5, 2011. http://www.christianitytoday.com/ct/2011/julyweb -only/francis-chan-hell.html. Accessed November 7, 2011.

8 Rob Bell, "Converts to Hell," Mars Hill Bible Church, Grandville, MI, October 14, 2007. Sermon. MP3.

dogmatic equations, but stories that enticed and drew people into a narrative. Based on Matthew 7:7, Bell showed that faith is sometimes like "asking," sometimes like "seeking," and sometimes like "knocking." For Bell, faith is precarious. Its true nature is more a verb than a noun: an intention toward God, rather than a claim about God.

As we saw previously, Bell inhabits the betwixt and between of everyday life, in which human passions for answers aren't always met with clarity—and, in fact, sometimes aren't met at all. Humans are sometimes stumped; doubts are confirmed. Bell implies that when preachers proclaim absolutes, they create "converts to hell." They make false promises and lead others into cul-de-sacs, where the contingencies of faith are short-circuited, avoided, and suppressed. "Perhaps in our evangelism," Bell reflects, "we ought to be a little more honest about the faith."

Bell continued by reading from Psalm 77, declaring that "half of all the psalms are forms of lament." The psalmists groan with unfulfilled desire, but "Jesus never says, come to God and all will be well." Bell was quick to explain that "ultimate reality is good, but it will take time." Bell refuses to promise certainty; he plays with ambiguity, pointing out that the interstices of human life complicate and often thwart the impulse for quick answers. The faithful must often surf across the swells and valleys that form the very topography of human experience. Otherwise, humans are met with suffering, which is unexpected and brutal—and they are left wondering: Is this what God promised?

Bell then moved to John 4—the meeting of Jesus and the Samaritan woman at the well. Here Jesus asks the woman for a drink, and the woman, who is suspect not only because of her ethnicity but also because she's alone and retrieving water in the middle of the day, rejects Jesus' request. Jesus responds by suggesting rather circuitously, "If you knew the gift of God and who it is that asks you for a drink, you would have asked him and he would have given you living water" (v. 4). In the end, Bell used this meeting with Jesus as yet another metaphor of the divine life: "Jesus is appealing to her deepest longings, and he likens it to thirst." When someone is thirsty, "water . . . is satisfying; it quenches our deepest thirst."

In rapid fire, Bell explained the story of Nicodemus, the teacher of the law. Responding to Jesus, Nicodemus exclaims, "Surely they cannot enter a second time into their mother's womb to be born!" (John 3:4). Bell imagined Jesus thinking, *"And this one is a teacher of the law?"* Enigmatically, Jesus responds, "You have to be born in water and spirit, the wind blows where it will you hear its sounds but you cannot tell where it comes from or where its going, so it is with everyone born of the spirit" (John 3:7-8, ESV). So God is like "a bit of wind, which blows." It is a mystery where it goes to and where it comes from.

In a set of four scriptures, Bell savages the idea that faith is a formula whereby one believes and is saved. Legalistic prescriptions of faith flatten the mystery of how humans actually respond to God. These prescriptions create blueprints of belief used to bludgeon opponents. They cripple thought and the imagination of the spirit's work in life. They simplify and reduce commitment to mere marks of membership. They undercut the complexity of a faithful response that Jesus implies in his interactions with followers. Life in faith is always more complex, rigorous, and mysterious than many assume—transformation in thought and action demands everything from the follower.

Faith, rather, is like someone "asking, seeking, knocking." Faith is like water that "quenches thirst." Faith is like wind that blows. It can't be controlled; it comes and goes. Even with faith—perhaps especially in faith—the question of certainty is no longer the point but rather a deep intention that involves no guarantees whatsoever. A desire not always fulfilled, a question not always answered. Bell concludes,

> There are no guarantees; I thought it would all work out.
> How many of you know exactly what I'm talking about? Jesus
> uses the image of wind. For some people, the spirit of God
> works in powerful ways; they become more and more com-

passionate and more and more filled with wisdom. The truth takes them over. They become a powerful light in dark places, and other people show up and experience a momentary time of joy and stay for two years. And then they're gone, and they want nothing to do with any of it. There aren't any guarantees. We know who Jesus is and what God is like, and beyond that, there are no guarantees.

As teacher and preacher, Bell uses what he finds in the teachings of Jesus to controvert coercive forms of evangelism that guarantee a doubt-free journey. He upturns views of faith that, in his opinion, misrepresent the exigencies of human experience in the day-to-day journey of faith. Faith in simplistic and dogmatic forms turns people toward a self-righteousness that breeds a Pharisaic attitude of arrogance and contempt. This kind of faith closes the mind and cripples the heart.

Is Bell mocking fundamentalist and legalistic evangelical Christians? Perhaps. He certainly puts them under a microscope and weighs them against his own interpretation of biblical and prophetic standards. In his early days at Mars Hill, Bell started out as a cocksure, charismatic evangelist. From there, he evolved into "the later Bell," who remains sure in his presentation but is far more subtle and conditional in his theological and pastoral approach.

For Bell, faith comes alive in the shadows of doubt, and heaven is more a presence than a destination. Bell puts all of these terms into play, and in fact argues that the coercion of certainty is itself the problem. Bell suggests that faith characterized in forms of certainty is akin to the religion of the Pharisees. For the authors of the gospels, it can't get any worse than that.

At the same time, Bell's detractors continue to build accusations against him: that Bell is watering down the faith, accommodating popular culture, and even weakening and diluting the force and righteousness of the gospel. Galli's book proclaims that "the Almighty doesn't need us to give him a face-lift and airbrush his image."[9] Chan,

9 See Mark Galli's *God Wins*, p. xi.

clearly responding to Bell, talks about his own need "to repent" for his attempt "to make God more palatable or attractive."[10]

But Bell is hardly an accommodator. He questions the Christian Right's allegiance to the American empire. He implies that solidarity with the poor is *the* way of discipleship. He neither marketed his church nor spent money on its facilities. He questioned the banal assurances of the prosperity gospel. And, after all, he published *Love Wins*. In doing so, he asked questions that he must have known would alienate him from many of his most loyal conservative audience and consumers.

Nevertheless, particularly in *Love Wins*, Bell downplays the judgment of God. Some accuse him of diminishing the consequences of human sinfulness. Both of these charges need to be understood in the wider context of Bell's work. What, then, is Bell's take on salvation and resurrection? Does Bell, in fact, believe in these fundamental propositions of Christian orthodoxy?

Disembodied Evacuation

The simple answer is yes. Across many of Bell's sermons there remains a consistent and simple declaration that "Jesus has risen! He has risen, indeed!" But, of course, nothing in religious faith is that simple. What do the life, death, and resurrection of Jesus Christ really mean? Bell's answer to this core question is where the argument begins for many evangelicals. Bell contends, "Resurrection does not mean some kind of disembodied evacuation to some other place. It's about this world, this life."[11] For Bell, resurrection is an affirmation and confirmation of God becoming human in Jesus Christ. The resurrection validates the incarnation and guarantees the hope and reality of the new creation that has started here and now—in this world—meaning that God's life is for this world. Bell documents the multiple appearances of Jesus to the disciples after his crucifixion. He

---

10 Mark Galli, "Q&A: Francis Chan on Rob Bell and Hell."

11 Rob Bell, "Resurrection," Mars Hill Bible Church, Grandville, MI, April 4, 2010. Sermon. MP3.

highlights the Apostle Paul's recollection of "hundreds" of witnesses, even decades later, continuing to report that Jesus appeared to them after his death and *in the flesh.*

Bell claims that the Gospel of John is a series of seven signs that culminate in an eighth sign, the resurrection; this resurrection marks the first day of the new creation. John's gospel ends with these words: "Jesus performed many other signs in the presence of his disciples, which are not recorded in this book. But these are written that you may believe that Jesus is the Messiah, the Son of God, and that by believing you may have life in his name" (John 20:30). Here, there is no mention of life after death, but "life" in this world, renewed in the resurrected Christ, making all things "new."[12]

The power of this notion overwhelms Bell. As he would say, it changes everything:

> There is a new creation, right here and right now. As a Christian you learn to see the new creation that is bursting forth right here and right now amidst us. It's about this world. The empty tomb, you didn't see that coming did ya? Resurrection is the affirmation of creation, bone and skin, cup and bread, the kiss and embrace, and God is rescuing it from the decay of destruction. Who we help matters. What we make matters. How we deal with the environment matters. What we believe matters. Resurrection gives us the resources to do something about the world. You go and do something about Haiti; you go and do something for your neighbor. You help your loved ones; you are inspired to keep going. The new creation matters.[13]

For many, this may not seem very controversial, and yet this radical immanence of the divine in the here and now is hotly debated. To many who have been educated in the subtleties of Christian

---

12 Rob Bell, "Beginning in the Beginning," Mars Hill cChurch, Grandville, MI, August 16, 2009. Sermon. MP3.

13 Rob Bell, "Resurrection."

theology, the basic promise of Christian faith *is* the hope of heaven in the world to come.

Thus, for many, Bell's most shocking claim—the reason that he *cannot* be right—is his assertion that "resurrection is not about somewhere else; it's about here." In *Surprised by Hope*, N.T. Wright argues along the same lines in a book that Bell blurbed: "The whole point of my argument so far is that the question of what happens to me after death is *not* the major, central framing question that centuries of theological tradition has supposed. The New Testament, true to its Old Testament roots, regularly insists that the major, central concern is God's purpose of rescue and re-creation for the whole world, the entire cosmos."[14] For Bell and for his followers, what is truly surprising is that this "good news" is so scandalous. For many evangelicals, Bell undercuts or downplays the future hope of Christianity and is attacking the very heart of their faith. The assumption is that faith is primarily about the world to come and each person's individual destiny. Many contemporary surveys about religion, particularly in Christian majority nations, ask the same set of questions, "Do you believe in heaven?" "Do you believe in hell?" Of course, many do, and, not surprisingly, most believe they (and their family and friends) are going to heaven (heaven being an actual place); most also believe in hell, but fewer than 1 percent believe they are going there. It is deeply internalized in the culture: Christ saves us for eternal life in heaven.[15]

When Bell says "NO!" he comes across as an outlier. Chan's, Galli's, and DeYoung's critiques of *Love Wins* challenge Bell's framework, arguing that he distorts the faith and gives "false hope" to

---

14 N.T. Wright, *Surprised by Hope*, p. 184.

15 Eighty-six percent of Americans believe in heaven, many believing that it is an "actual place." Two thirds of Americans believe they are going to heaven. Seventy-three percent of Americans believe in hell, but less than one percent believe they are going there. See Mark Chaves' *American Religion: Contemporary Trends*, p. 33. See also the Barna Group, "Americans Describe their Views About Life After Death," 2009. http://www.barna.org/barna-update/article/5-barna-update/128-americans-describe-their-views-about-life-after-death?q=heaven+hell. Accessed April 5, 2012.

Christians. They believe Bell deceives Christians about the truth of the end. They assert that the judgment of God *is* coming and that, when it comes, heaven or hell are the only options. DeYoung, in particular, insists that Bell's theory of the atonement is not only deficient but also distorted; that is, "Bell completely ignores the theory of penal substitution."

The phrase *penal substitution* is hardly common but absolutely crucial in the neo-Reformed evangelical community. Because of the force of human sin, Reformed theology asserts that a holy and just God demands a perfect sacrifice. That sacrifice is Jesus Christ, who pays the price for sin and earns redemption for humankind. By faith in Christ, humanity has grace "imputed" as a legal decree. The death and resurrection of Jesus Christ wins salvation and eternal life for those who claim Christ's name. But for those who resist this gift, God has no choice but to send them to hell.

This is precisely the Christian story that Bell parodies in *Love Wins.* This vision of God is unacceptable to Bell, particularly in light of the gospels and the parables of Jesus:

> Millions have been taught that if they don't believe, if they don't accept in the right way, that is, the way the person telling them the gospel does, and they were hit by a car and died later that same day, God would have no choice but to punish them forever in conscious torment in hell. God would, in essence, become a fundamentally different being to them in that moment of death, a different being to them forever. A loving, heavenly father who will go to extraordinary lengths to have a relationship with them would, in the blink of an eye, become a cruel, mean, vicious tormenter who would insure that they would have no escape from an endless future of agony.[16]

And, for Bell, this kind of God doesn't make sense, "If there was an earthly father who was like that, we would call the authorities.

---

16 Rob Bell, *Love Wins*, pp. 173-174.

If there was an actual human dad who was that volatile, we would contact child protection services immediately."[17] Here Bell attacks the very heart of neo-Reformed theology: the assumption that because of the nature of human sin, humans are unacceptable in the sight of a holy God. Bell finds this logic utterly strange: If God is in Jesus Christ reconciling the world to himself, how can punishment trump mercy, judgment defeat grace, and retribution undermine forgiveness? Bell believes God will not go against God's very nature, for as Bell recalls in the psalms, "The mercies of God are everlasting."[18]

DeYoung responds to Bell's parody of the neo-Reformed God by arguing, "Of course, this is a horrible caricature that makes God seem capricious and vindictive. No one I know thinks God is loving one minute and cruel the next. But God is always holy. And holy love is not the same as unconditional affirmation. Holy love is more terrifying than even Bell thinks and more unbelievably merciful and free than Bell imagines." This radical paradox of a Holy God who is unconditionally loving and radically just is the core of neo-Reformed theology. Humans deserve damnation because God is holy, but in fact God is all loving. So, through the sacrifice of Christ, humans are "saved," and their sentence is overturned. This gift is both unconditional and unearned. The good news of this pronouncement is precisely the notion that, in Christ, an objective form of salvation has been given, without condition or earned merit. Humans who proclaim Jesus is Lord accept this gift and are saved.

Many demur from this construction of the story of salvation, but any fair-minded person can understand why such a formulation is so powerful. The absolute assurance of salvation from God in Christ, regardless of the nature of one's sin, generates a deep sense of reassurance, if not confidence. More to the point, the scriptures overflow with portraits of a holy God who demands righteousness and levies punishment when these demands are not met. As a result,

---

17 Rob Bell, *Love Wins*, p. 174.
18 Rob Bell's paraphrase of Psalm 100:5

many Christians have no doubt that Bell downplays God's holiness and judgment.

Is DeYoung correct, then, in accusing Bell of creating "a different God"? This seems to be the core indictment for most critics. Bell avoids the parts of the scripture that present a God whom he finds unappealing. As DeYoung elegantly summarizes: "If anything, one might mention that the only thrice-repeated attribute [for God] is 'holy, holy, holy.' And yet this is the one thing Bell's god is not. Having preached through Leviticus he should remember that holiness is the overarching theme. The sacrifices are a pleasing aroma in God's nostrils because they satisfy his justice, making way for a holy God to dwell in the midst of an unholy people. That Christ's sacrifice is the same pleasing aroma to God (Eph. 5:2) undercuts Bell's insistence that God did not need to rescue us from God." DeYoung argues, fairly, that within this picture of salvation there is a powerful dynamic of judgment and acquittal. Scripture insists that "all fall short of the glory of God" (Rom 3:23), and yet, in God's mercy, salvation has been won because of Christ's sacrifice on the cross. The conviction of this paradox is powerful to many.

Yet for some, the penal substitution model is a legalistic, grotesque parody of God's infinite love. Does Bell make a plausible argument that this equation necessarily creates a "volatile" and abusive portrait of God? Does the neo-Reformed insistence on the theory of penal substitution of the atonement distort the meaning of salvation? And to be sure, this is a core question for believers who line up on various sides of this issue—a kind of litmus test for the neo-Reformed, and a test that, to them, Bell fails. Thus, we can understand the reason for the ferocity of the attack against him and *Love Wins,* in particular.

Sacrifice as a Pleasing Aroma

Within the conservative Reformed movement, to deny the penal substitution theory of the atonement marks a person as truly outside the boundaries of evangelical faith. This logical sequence accounts for this model of salvation:

- God is holy.
- God demands holiness.
- People are imperfect.
- Because they are imperfect, people sin.
- God is just.
- Because God is just, God requires payment for sin.
- In God's infinite compassion, God gave Jesus as a perfect sacrifice.
- Jesus' crucifixion produces the "pleasing aroma" and atones for human sin.
- And in God's infinite mercy, salvation is won, and the resurrection of Jesus Christ is the final victory for all who are in Christ, forever and eternally.

This is a powerful theory of salvation for millions of Christians, but widening the lens, three other theories of the doctrine of atonement enjoy a similar level of adherence within the wider Christian tradition.

The first is the *exemplary* theory, which argues that Jesus' death is both an ultimate submission to God's will and a heroic portrayal of Jesus' faithfulness toward humankind. Thus, the love of God is exemplified through Jesus Christ. In this way, Jesus' "death is not a transaction but an inspiration."[19]

For the Church Fathers and throughout the first millennium of Christian history, the *Christus Victor* theory of atonement reigned supreme. In this theory, the death of Christ represents God's ultimate defeat of evil, along with sin and death. "Jesus' death is a moment of active resistance to evil."[20] Fear, sin, and death rule over the lives of all humankind, but through Christ humanity is released from these powers.

The third theory emanates from the doctrine of the *incarnation* itself, "The divine nature is infused into humanity, and Christ is . . .

---

19 Mark S. Heim, *Saved from Sacrifice: A Theology of the Cross.* Grand Rapids, MI: William B. Eerdmans Publishing Company, 2006, p. 5.

20 Mark S. Heim, *Saved from Sacrifice,* p. 5.

this healing power [that] radiates in the bloodstream of our collective human nature."[21] The life, death, and resurrection of Christ form a healing stream for humanity, inspiring the moral life, conquering death, resisting evil, and instigating the new creation in the world itself, as a "foretaste" of the "abundant life" given by the spirit and the life to come in the kingdom of God.

The penal substitution theory of atonement is a fourth theory, codified by Anselm in the eleventh century. The theory never developed in the Eastern Orthodox Church, in part because the Orthodox tradition rejected Augustine's doctrine of original sin. Nonetheless, it became a crucial building block and core doctrine to the Protestant Reformers, Martin Luther and John Calvin. This theory of atonement imagines a God who demands a sacrifice for the offense of human sin. And thus the question, "What does this theory say about the nature of God itself?"

Bell's *Love Wins* goes to the heart of this question: Precisely what kind of God do Christians worship? Is it a God whose anger must be appeased, a God whose mercy must be revealed, or a God whose justice must be served? Many would argue all three, and would suggest that maintaining this tension is precisely what creates the powerful paradox of Christian salvation. To be sure, over one thousand passages document God's rage toward humanity and God's willingness to destroy them.[22] The God of scripture embodies, at times, a fierce judgment and an intense jealousy. How do Christians negotiate the expressions of God's anger with the love powerfully portrayed in the words of Jesus' Sermon on the Mount?

Was Jesus the ultimate sacrifice? Bell believes that Christ's sacrifice is not for God's sake. Rather, it is the ultimate revelation of the innocent victim, the final scapegoat. René Girard's theory of scapegoating illumines how Bell negotiates this knotty problem. Girard

---

21 Mark S. Heim, *Saved from Sacrifice*, p. 6.

22 See Mark S. Heim, *Saved from Sacrifice*, p. 68. For a broad discussion of the more violent portrayals of God, see Regina Schwartz's *The Curse of Cain: The Violent Legacy of Monotheism*. Chicago, IL: University of Chicago Press, 1998.

argues that through the prophets, God said, "I desire mercy, not sacrifice, and acknowledgment of God rather than burnt offerings" (Hos 6:6). Abraham, who lifted his hand to sacrifice his son Isaac, had his hand stayed by God. The God of the Hebrews is the one who puts a stop to sacrifice in the religions of the Near East. Going even further, the Hebrew God reveals that sacrifice is nothing more than a form of human scapegoating, which destroys the weak in order to mitigate social unrest and to reset patterns of human community.[23]

Girard asserts the claim, that Jesus' death is the ultimate revelation of the scapegoat's innocence. His death reveals the need and necessity to end the scapegoating process. His death is not demanded by God, but made necessary to reveal the folly of humanity and the necessity to begin to love and forgive the enemy.

Contemporary Reformed theologian Mark Heim argues that "Jesus' death saves the world, and it ought not to happen. It's God's plan and an evil act. It is a good bad thing."[24] It is necessary, because the scapegoating mechanism must be revealed for what it is, a barbaric act of evil. In this way, Jesus "unmasks" the sacrificial system once and for all, and judges the system for what it is—an evil act of scapegoating the innocent and vulnerable.

Yet many evangelicals claim, "Yes, but God is holy and demands recompense for human sin." Galatians 3:13 stipulates that "Christ redeemed us . . . by becoming a curse for us," (CEB) and there are many other passages that also refer to God's holiness and the need for reconciliation. In the face of such interpretations Bell asks: If God is the one who demands blood sacrifice, how is God any different from any human ruler who demands revenge and a scapegoat to control the conflicts among God's constituents? Does this not lower God to the same level as any *human* despot?

---

23 See René Girard's *Things Hidden from the Foundation of the World.* Translated by Stephen Bann and Michael Metteer. Stanford, CA: Stanford University Press, 1987.

24 Mark S. Heim, *Saved from Sacrifice,* p. 108.

For Bell, the words *and* actions of Jesus settle this dispute, once and for all. The call in Christ is to give up the sacrificial system and to stop the normal methods of mediating human conflict expressed as an "eye for an eye." Bell quotes Jesus' powerful words against this system in the Sermon on the Mount: "Blessed are the meek. . . . Blessed are the peacemakers. . . . Blessed are those who are persecuted because of righteousness, for theirs is the kingdom of heaven. . . . You have heard that it was said, 'Love your neighbor and hate your enemy.' But I tell you, love your enemies and pray for those who persecute you." (Matt 5:5-43). Bell believes the religion of Jesus Christ is a religion that identifies with the scapegoat, which refuses to use the mechanism of sacrifice. In fact, sacrifice is the problem, and the scapegoat is the victim with whom the follower of Jesus must identify.[25]

The violent language in the scriptures *is*, however, a problem. And Bell asserts it must be confronted, particularly in a day and time when violence is often a function of religious conflict.[26] And while sin separates the human from the divine for Bell, it is not God's doing—for in Christ, God forgives and seeks to redeem the sinner and reconcile them to himself. Bell holds that God doesn't instigate violence but redeems it, opening the doors to a new humanity. Furthermore, Bell holds that God not only opens the door—but opens the door to all.

Christian Universalism?

Neither in *Love Wins* nor anywhere else does Bell use the term *universalism*. Bell argues that he doesn't use it because it "means too

---

25 Mark S. Heim, *Saved from Sacrifice*, "The death of Jesus follows the script of human persecution because that is the ongoing evil into whose path Jesus steps, to rescue us from sacrifice, to open the way to new community," p. 301.

26 See my own work on religious violence, which shows how religious violence is prevalent in all religious traditions, across time, *Belief and Bloodshed: Religion and Violence across Time and Tradition*. Lanham, MD: Rowman & Littlefield, 2007.

many things to different people."[27] Again, for Bell, labels distort and alienate rather than clarify and illuminate matters of salvation. Nonetheless, in *Love Wins* he places his thinking about Christian salvation at the heart of the tradition: "And so, beginning with the early church, there is a long tradition of Christians who believe that God will ultimately restore everything and everybody, because Jesus says in Matthew 19 that there will be a 'renewal of all things.' Peter says in Acts 3 that Jesus will 'restore everything,' and Paul says in Colossians 1 that through Christ 'God was pleased to . . . reconcile to himself all things, whether things on earth or things in heaven.'"[28] And while these passages are in scripture, salvation as the reconciliation of all things—meaning the universal salvation of all through Christ—is a subordinate theme in Christian history. Most famously, Origen extolled this idea but was condemned for it. Augustine denounced it and, in the West, Aquinas, Luther, and Calvin assumed many were destined for hell.

At the same time, the Eastern Fathers of the Church (Clement of Alexandria, Gregory of Nyssa, Gregory of Nazianzen, Theodore of Mopsuestia, Evagrius Ponticus, and Maximus the Confessor) were sympathetic to the restoration of all things. The Eastern Church never accepted Augustine's doctrine of original sin. There was renewed interest in the Eastern Fathers by many Western theologians in the twentieth century led in part by the Swiss Reformed theologian Karl Barth and the Jesuit Hans Urs von Balthasar, a friend of Barth's. Balthasar's *Dare We Hope That All Men Are Saved?*[29] did not teach that all are certainly saved, which would deprive people of free will, but that Christians should live in the hope that all are saved. In this sense, Bell's work falls within a broader stream of the Christian tradition—one that has become more central to Christian thinking in the modern period.

---

27 Interview with Rob Bell by author, March 28, 2012.
28 Rob Bell, *Love Wins*, p. 107.
29 See Balthasar's *Dare We Hope that All Men Be Saved? With a Short Discourse on Hell.* San Francisco: Ignatius Press, 1988.

Bell is quick to assert that he believes in the existence of hell, but he is much less certain about how long it lasts and whether those who dwell there are there forever. This line of reasoning is one of the core theses of *Love Wins*: "At the center of the Christian tradition since the first church has been the insistence that history is not tragic, hell is not forever, and love, in the end, wins"[30]

This was not a new thought for Bell. Even in his first book, *Velvet Elvis*, Bell claimed something similar, "Heaven is full of forgiven people. Hell is full of forgiven people. Heaven is full of people God loves, whom Jesus died for. Hell is full of forgiven people God loves, whom Jesus died for. The difference is how we choose to live, which story we choose to live in, which version of reality we trust."[31] Bell is, and always has been, eager to rethink the Christian story that portrays God as holding billions of souls in some sort of fiery prison in which those who have rejected God's grace are eternally tortured. Without stating it, Bell implies a form of purgatory, a Catholic dogma that has long been rejected by Protestants. The doctrine of purgatory, however, provides a solution to many Christian dilemmas. It can be argued that purgatory is the only way one can have a God who is both just and merciful, while maintaining human free will.

Bell clearly holds out for the possibility of a postmortem second chance. He hopes, but doesn't insist, that those who have rejected God and are in hell will get one last shot at salvation. He lifts up various traditions to make his case, but without significant Protestant groundwork to buttress his claims. Bell moves against the mainstream—unless the reader turns to the Catholic tradition of purgatory, whereby sin is punished though not for eternity, and humans can continue to choose to repent, thus allowing for human choice and displaying a merciful God in time and through eternity.

Those who staunchly argue that hell is "conscious torture" for eternity make a bold and historically traditional case, but the debate will no doubt continue. For some evangelicals, including Mark Galli, the

---

30 Rob Bell, *Love Wins*, p. 109.
31 Rob Bell, *Velvet Elvis*, p. 146.

biblical evidence for conscious torture is far from certain. Galli offers the case, using the formula of *annihilationism,* that the human rejection of God ends in the total obliteration of the person as such, including the very image of God in the self. To be sure, a punishment of conscious torture by a loving God becomes even more suspect in light of the fact that torture is now considered a global crime against humanity.

René Girard's work on redemptive violence penetrates to the heart of this issue. The cross of Christ is not a confirmation of the need for "divine sadism" but a revelation of the evil of scapegoating and the need to overcome the human tendency to valorize the sacrificial system: "Our increasing discomfort with the cross is itself an effect of the cross. Far from being a rationalization of redemptive violence, the passion accounts definitively undermine it."[32]

That Bell has brought these issues to the fore—concerns that have precedence in the historical tradition as well as in scripture—not only underlines their critical nature for our understanding of Christian salvation but also suggests that these questions have consequences affecting how Christians negotiate matters of war and peace, life and death, and revenge and forgiveness. What we believe about atonement or reconciliation has moral consequences in this world.

Heaven on Earth

For Bell, a theology that focuses narrowly on the salvation of the soul makes the implicit claim that what we do in this world is largely unimportant. Our only significant decision is *for or against* Christ. Bell believes this creates a form of what he calls "evacuation theology," which denigrates the creation and undercuts how we live and have our being in this world. It breeds a discontent for what we have here and now. According to Bell:

What we do here, matters.

What we make here, matters.

How we serve here, matters.

---

32 Mark S. Heim, *Saved from Sacrifice,* p. 11.

If it is only about our destiny in the world to come, this world becomes a mere means to our true end; every person merely an object of evangelism. Not only do we instrumentalize each other, but also the world becomes a kind of wrecking ball from which we must be rescued.

The world, asserts Bell, is the field of our salvation; it is the stage for the kingdom of God. This promise is not a matter of denying the biblical revelation, but a reality that the scriptures illumine when read in their full Jewish context, and in the setting of the promises of God. The covenant is fulfilled in the book of Revelation in the marriage of heaven and earth, "God's dwelling place is now among the people" (Rev 21:3). God abides with humankind, promising to make "everything new" (Rev 21:5).

And, isn't that good news? To Bell and those who share his vision, it is *the* Good News. N.T. Wright is among those who have proclaimed that this news is as surprising as it is good. Wright argues forcefully, that to "see the death of the body and the escape of the soul as salvation is not simply slightly off course, in need of a few subtle alterations and modifications. It is totally and utterly wrong. It is colluding with death. It is conniving at death's destruction of God's good, image-bearing human creatures while consoling ourselves with the (essentially non-Christian and non-Jewish) thought that that really important bit of ourselves is saved from this wicked, nasty body and this sad, dark world of space, time, and matter!"[33] Even before reading Wright, Bell held this core conviction. This world is where the action is, and it has always been about this world. The kingdom of God is the metaphor Jesus uses to describe this terrain, and the parables of Jesus are the images that guide thought and action in line with the principles of this kingdom.

The church is not a loading station for heaven but a workshop into which people come to investigate, experiment, taste the abundant life, and be equipped to become witnesses. Mission is not a message given but a life lived; there is no ticket for another world. It

---

33 N.T. Wright, *Surprised by Hope*, p. 194. (Italics, author emphasis.)

is a life pressed into God's ecstatic power that produces what is true, good, and beautiful in this world. Life becomes a platform that is set for God's entrance: "They will be his people, and God himself will be with them and be their God" (Rev 21:3). As Wright puts it, "What you *do* in the present—by painting, preaching, singing, sewing, praying, teaching, building hospitals, digging wells, campaigning for justice, writing poems, caring for the needy, loving your neighbor as yourselves—*will last into God's future.*"[34]

Bell beckons those who preach and teach to recognize that in the resurrection of Jesus Christ, the new creation has begun; it reverses the pull of sin and reengineers the desires of the heart. It reorients persons toward inhabiting their gifts and talents for the common good; it transforms private interest into public benefit.

Bell, however, is no naïf. He understands that sin destroys the order of creation and is a form of rebellion against that order. And for Bell sin is personal—the distortion of how we act toward each other and ourselves—but it is also corporate and structural. That is, as a human community we have the resources to feed the world, and yet we don't: "Sin is a way [of] taking creation in an improper direction. Right now there are 800 million people who are starving, and we should find this number offensive. . . . [T]here is enough food to feed everybody in the world. The earth produces enough food, but the food has not been properly distributed. We have disrupted the shalom that God intends."[35] This is what angers God, says Bell, when God's good order is disrupted, and the good that we produce instead of creating shalom is confiscated and stored when it could be used to keep nearly a billion people alive. So, yes, God's judgment against this disorder is real, but it is also crystal clear in Bell's estimation what must be done. Rather than pining for heaven, the people of God must call individuals not only to change their hearts and lives but also to see how their obligation and destiny are inextricably attached to the needs of people everywhere.

---

34 N.T. Wright, *Surprised by Hope*, p. 193.
35 Rob Bell, "Beginning in the Beginning."

There is no distinction anymore between the good news and what the good news does on behalf of the world. As N.T. Wright explains, "Once we get the resurrection straight, we can and must get the mission straight."[36] The church's mission is to announce the inauguration of the new creation even now—the "kingdom always coming," in the words of Walter Rauschenbusch. This peace, fullness, and joy is greater than words and deeper than any doctrine or belief, because it is the power of resurrection creating new life in all things, giving new hope to all people, and providing provisions to feed the soul and body of everyone, everywhere.

In the last years of his ministry at Mars Hill, Bell's central argument was this: if one begins the story of salvation with the fall of Adam and Eve in Genesis 3 "then the primary story becomes about sin, people are sinners, and how do we get rid of this sin problem."[37] Jesus becomes the answer; he gets people forgiven. When the story starts with Genesis 3, the center of the plot is a sinful humanity in need of forgiveness. It is a story about how to get out of this world to heaven, and the action is somewhere else. But Bell insists, "If you begin in Gen 1, it's telling people what they are. You are a daughter and a son of an all loving and forgiving God, who creates and says that you are good. You are made in the image of this God. You are created to be a co-creator with God in moving creation forward to ever increasing dimensions of shalom. God is now standing on his tiptoes, waiting and inviting you home to return to who you are."[38] Bell's hope, then, is rooted not so much in a human drive but in a divine promise, in the death and resurrection of Jesus Christ.

This divine action is the primary engine of human hope—a hope that is a new creation, resisting evil, defeating death, and creating pathways so humans may flourish in talents that express themselves in a life-giving force for others. "Our hope is rooted in engagement, not in escape but in reclamation. It's about staying and not leaving.

---

36 N.T. Wright, *Surprised by Hope*, p. 193.
37 Rob Bell, "Beginning in the Beginning."
38 Rob Bell, "Beginning in the Beginning."

Christians are never surprised that truth, meaning, and goodness show up in all sorts of unexpected places, because it is God's world, it always has been God's world, and it will always be God's world."[39]

Love wins then in the sense that God's will is the reconciliation of all things—the soul, the body, the earth, the cosmos, and everything in it. But contrary to what some argue—that Bell's vision is human-centric—this is God's action, and this action is centered on making a heaven of earth. Bell's hope is that all people will eventually join in this great dance, but he also knows that God forces no one. In the Parable of the Ten Virgins five virgins are ready, and they join a party in progress; five aren't ready, and they are caught outside this "epic party." In his sermon on this passage, Bell paints a magnificent picture of heaven on earth, but cautions that human destiny remains in our hands. Bell hopes for a second chance for all people, but he warns, "The truth is, kids grow up, bodies fail, some opportunities pass, and you don't get a second chance. So this parable is about readiness today. Is there anything that you have been putting off, and the strong, compelling, beautiful, word of Jesus is this: you do not have tomorrow, you have today."[40]

Bell endlessly shows God's mercy and God's longing to make all things—all people—new. But there are times when he gently but firmly warns that it is time to change and move away from addictions and forms of dehumanization; time to focus on the needs of the world rather than hoard our abundance; time to share what we have, and care for the billions of humans who hunger and thirst. Love might win, but to do so humans must respond. The burden and urgency to choose, remains.

---

39 Rob Bell, "Beginning in the Beginning."
40 Rob Bell, "Ten Virgins," Mars Hill Bible Church, Grandville, MI, November 14, 2010. Sermon. MP3.

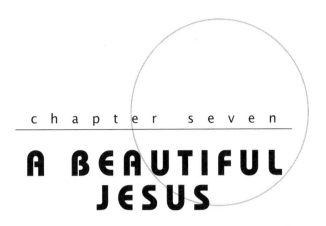

chapter   seven

A BEAUTIFUL
JESUS

*"The downside of humanity is becoming all wrapped up in yourself
and not remembering and understanding who you serve. But if you want to
go somewhere else because you feel you're apostolic, Hollywood is the launching
pad for porn and for greatness. It doesn't serve any master above the other. If
they can make money at it, they'll do it; it doesn't matter what it is.
So, it's really an opportunity of a lifetime."*

A close associate commenting on Bell's move to Hollywood.[1]

When Bell resigned from Mars Hill with rumors of Hollywood waiting in the wing, an onrush of opinions and reactions ensued. From
immediate dismissal, "Oh, he must be a fraud," or, "Wow, he must
be looking for a big paycheck," to cynicism about his religion, "Yep,
he's given up on his faith and his church." While an abiding suspicion of Hollywood courses through the American religious landscape, Bell's Mars Hill friends and associates had a different response.
Yes, Hollywood is the purveyor of "porn," but it's also the launching

---

1 Interview with Rob Bell associate by author, November 19, 2011.

pad of "greatness." Some understood Bell's decision as going into the belly of the beast. Admittedly, he whiffed on his first swing, with the failure of his TV show *Stronger* to be piloted, but his confidence did not waiver. Bell has been responsible for a stunning series of successes, ranging from raising a megachurch from scratch to producing a range of well-known and highly regarded publications and films. With this history of achievements to bolster him, he continues to pursue his calling: ultimately, to "compellingly share the gospel." Where better than Hollywood? Bell's next release is scheduled to be a TV show with spiritual and religious content that would feature the faith that he had always wanted to share with ever-larger audiences. How it will be received is still up in the air. It's as big a risk as he has ever taken, but the knife-edge of that gamble also carries the promise of an extraordinary reward.

Bell could have stayed at his church, preached the gospel, and built a secure cathedral to surround him while he sowed the word of God into the thousands of people he served. But his desire to live a life that he had written and preached about called for risk and innovation. His repeated mantra has been, "What do I have to lose?"

More importantly, Bell promised to do something that had never been done before: "to create a place in the middle of culture for a really beautiful Jesus." This is after all Bell's dream, and everything he has done before leads to this moment. "I want to show it to you, when everyone else is having a conference about how to present Jesus to the world, I want to do it, in the belly of the beast, a beautiful Jesus and people will say, 'Wow.'"

What fascinates so many about Bell is that it has been tough to nail him down. He seems not to fit very well in either the evangelical or liberal camps. And this is perhaps what is most appealing about him. There has been a steady decline in American mainline Protestant churches, and more recently in many of the traditional evangelical denominations, including the Southern Baptist Convention. Americans are tired of the religious wars between evangelicals and liberals, but they never tire of Jesus and his way. The question remains how to present it to a wider public in the midst of an American audience transfixed by *The Bachelorette, Keeping up with the Kardashians,* and *Family Guy.* Is there room for a beautiful Jesus in the midst of our present day media?

So, in this midterm evaluation of Bell's life and work we look not only at his legacy but also at how he might be plowing a new American Christianity. Some say he's apostolic—a spiritual charismatic; others call him a spiritual virtuoso—a man who represents spirit in the world. Whatever his guise, one might wonder in what ways he is a harbinger—a representative of what is coming in the future for American Christian faith.

Bell and the American Religious Menagerie

Two recent books about American Christianity make distinct cases for its future. In *Bad Religion,* Ross Douhat argues that America is a land of "heretics," and calls for a return to a type of Christian orthodoxy.[2] In *Christianity after Religion,* Diane Butler Bass frames Christianity as moving into a new day—one that is spiritual but not religious, devout without need for the church. Bell's call to a gospel, which is a Jewish-rooted and Jesus-centered faith, makes him seem almost obtuse.[3] Both books note the hybrid nature of American religion and Christianity—the former wanting to reign in this tendency, the latter celebrating the fissiparous nature of American spirituality.

The reality is that American religion is a religious menagerie.[4] Historically, that has been the case, and its future looks consistently aligned. Mark Silk divides American religion up into eight distinct regional enclaves. But even within these there is tremendous heterogeneity, and the regions continue to change over time. Think of the Northeast and Massachusetts, in particular. Though Boston

---

2 See Douhat's *Bad Religion: How We Became a Nation of Heretics.* NY: Free Press, 2012.

3 See Bass's *Christianity after Religion: End of Church and the Birth of a New Spiritual Awakening.* NY: Harper-Collins Publishers, 2012.

4 See Silk's and Walsh's *One Nation, Divisible.*

was the birthplace of the American Puritans, Roman Catholics now dominate that landscape of faith. Moreover, Massachusetts' governor from 2003–2007 was a Mormon who became the Republican Party's nominee for President of the United States in 2012. Only a generation ago such a thing wouldn't have been possible. American Christianity is a hybrid species whose ability to splinter and fragment has only increased over time. The many factions that argue for a return to some mythical Christian purity fail to understand this historical perspective; their faith is no more orthodox than what it is trying to replace. This country truly is the home of heretics—staunch religious individualists who refuse to bow to any one way to practice the faith.

Two larger changes, however, are having a major impact on American religion. One is the way Americans think about religion, and the second is how they structure their churches. The majority of Americans, for the first time in our history, now believe Christianity isn't the only true faith.[5] And, in the last forty years, megachurches have become the dominant mode of Christian worship for nearly half of all churchgoers. Americans are now more pluralistic and tolerant in their views on religious difference; they also are much less loyal to a specific brand of Christianity. They tend to rally around larger churches that mostly avoid denominational affiliations or even specific Christian theological traditions.

The American church today is more like a Costco outlet store that serves a generic form of Christianity with all sorts of different benefits added on—entertainment for kids, therapeutic outlets for people at almost every stage of their lives, various products and media to be purchased, and star performers who have become regional and sometimes national and international celebrities. Some criticize this as mere consumerist religion, but megachurch-goers rate their churches very high on spiritual growth.[6] Americans are going to these large churches because they receive a great deal from them. These evangelical churches also provide and challenge churchgoers

---

5 See Mark Chaves' *American Religion: Contemporary Trends.*
6 See my forthcoming book *High on God.*

to give and serve in ways that have been shown to far outdo their smaller, liberal church counterparts.[7] It is into this setting that Rob Bell plies his trade. But the questions remain: Is Bell an evangelical, or is he a liberal—a social gospel type? These questions motivated many of my own queries to him as I prodded and pushed him for a clear response. What emerged was his refusal to bite down on any one label. More interesting was his refusal to see himself as a leader of a movement. And this antipathy to movement labels extended to his theological vision. Bell explained, "In my experience, whatever label you use to label God, the God that you are after will always be bigger."[8] For Bell, the God we construct is always too small.

Bell clarified his own allergy to labels by pointing to 1 Corinthians 3:21–23, which he described as having a huge impact on him[9]: "So then, no more boasting about human leaders! All things are yours, whether Paul or Apollos or Cephas or the world or life or death or the present or the future—all are yours, and you are of Christ, and Christ is of God." To label God, or to stop exploring the multifarious aspects of God, is a dead-end pursuit—a category implosion and, in the end, self-defeating.

To ask Bell whether he is an evangelical or a liberal is beside the point. On traditional evangelical perspectives, Bell disputes whether the phrase "personal relationship with God" is even biblical. He sees scripture as inspired, but the category of inerrancy makes little sense to him. He has called for conversion to Christ but has also made clear that it comes to each person uniquely and should come without coercion. He seems socially conservative generally, rarely making his stances explicit. Abortion is a moral choice, which should remain legal, but it should also be rare. On the ever-controversial issue of homosexuality—a litmus test for many evangelicals *and*

---

7 See my *Evangelicals vs. Liberals: The Clash of Christian Cultures in the Pacific Northwest* for how to distinguish these two types of Christianities.

8 Interview with Rob Bell by author, March 28, 2012.

9 Interview with Rob Bell by author, March 28, 2012.

liberals—sources say he has always been open on the issue. Though when directly asked about it, he never declared himself in one camp or another.

What is central for Bell is the dynamism of the spirit of God that he experiences as the kingdom of God catalyzing his creativity and calling him to make things and do acts of mercy and justice. From this inner vitality comes Bell's spirit of creativity and compassion. In light of this, for him, *evangelical* and *liberal* are labels that inhibit rather than illumine the living nature of the gospel.

Bell's Legacy and Challenge

Creative types shun convention. Bell's whole career is a series of moments in which he challenges expectations, ignores critics, and goes his own way, trusting the voice of his spirit and conscience—rattling some and intriguing others.

Bell is no fan of church structure or administration, but this may be more a function of his personal idiosyncrasies than a deep-seated philosophical principle. When asked if he thinks the church is necessary for faith, Bell responded, "Developmentally, the church should be a catalyst for the kingdom of God; it awakens and aligns us." But this catalyzing process is just that—a dynamic that motivates and points towards the goal of healing, forgiving, and doing compassion and justice in the world. Bell was quick to explain, "We gather together, but if we stay together too long we'll start creating a separate thing and start working against the thing we wanted to do in the first place."[10]

Humans tend to cling to structures and associations that bring comfort, but too often they then seek forms of permanence to defend and hold as absolutes. More often than not, Bell has intentionally fought against this tendency, making suggestions to the Mars Hill community, such as, "Why don't we move every two years so nobody gets too used to the place?" He didn't create a permanent

---

10 Interview with Rob Bell by author, March 28, 2012.

base for his church; he also didn't tear down the old, dilapidated mall where Mars Hill remains. He simply painted the walls, set up chairs and a stage and screen, and said, "Let's worship." Clinging to permanence, for Bell, must be avoided. The point is not the place but the purpose of the kingdom—to live into a compassionate, justice seeking, and creative type of faith life.

Bell insists that the "church is the mission." The church shouldn't be in the business of farming out mission. It should become the arms and hands of service in the place in which it exists. Mars Hill became a powerful agency of mission not only in Grand Rapids but also, through the ingenuity of the congregation, in Africa, where it helped to transform deserts into springs by creating wells that produced clean water for thousands.

In tandem with this belief, Bell holds that all Christians are, by definition, *the* missionaries of the church. Bell refused to advertise his church. There were no signs on the old mall, and the only way one might know it was a church was because somebody, by word of mouth, told new people, "Come to Mars Hill." By refusing to market the church through traditional measures, Bell encouraged Mars Hill members to be the people who told the story of how they had become alive in the kingdom of God. On any number of occasions, Bell explained that when somebody would proudly announce to Bell, "I'm thinking about full-time Christian ministry," he would always ask, "Are you a Christian?" If they answered in the affirmative, he would then follow with, "It's too late, you already *are* in full-time ministry."

This push to dethrone missionaries as special or as set apart challenged people to take responsibility for their faith. As Bell pronounced many times, "Ordain everyone in the church." By redefining what it means to be in mission, Mars Hill members came face to face with the responsibility of taking the church out into their everyday lives. For Bell's congregation, there was no one else to pass this task onto.

Bell also took the risk and entered the fray, creating a direct challenge to contemporary American Christianity, asking whether it was actually faith or justice that motivated Americans to endorse the American empire and its sense of entitlement and security. With critical and calculated comments about the Iraq War, he gained critics on both sides of the issue. When he asked if we are protecting people or just the resources that make our "lifestyle" possible, he was also asking a question that other evangelicals had asked as well. Greg Boyd, a fellow evangelical megachurch pastor, lost a significant percentage of his church members because of his criticism of the Iraq War.[11] Both Bell and Boyd made the claim that seeking to be faithful to the scriptures means following a God who is in solidarity not with great empires of history but with the victims of those empires.

As Bell would often say, more than half the world lives on much less than what the poorest Americans live on. How does that correlate with the American entitlement that assumes the American lifestyle is our right as a nation—an inalienable right? Both the Old and New Testaments make clear that God is close to "the orphan and the widow," so for Bell the idea that God favors the rich is a distortion of scripture, a false sense that wealth is a right and not a gift, killing the very joy that defines the essence of the gift in the first place.

Bell asserts that the notion that God's central goal is each person's security fundamentally undercuts the necessity of risk in discipleship. Bell often announced the mission of Mars Hill as "a disciple making disciples, making disciples. . . ." The only thing important is to mentor people to follow Christ, and to make *this* the aim and goal of everything one does. Through scripture the goal of discipleship is solidarity not only with the poor and the dispossessed but also with that which is good, beautiful, and true in the world.

Bell centers his spiritual and religious ideas on the power and motivating force of the kingdom of God—Jesus' central focus. Bell uses the metaphor of the kingdom as the key to his incarnational theology, suggesting that Jesus is God's Son in the world who

---

11 See Greg A. Boyd's *The Myth of a Christian Nation.*

inaugurates and introduces his followers to the kingdom of God, which is a dynamic reality in the present moment and not only as promise that is to come. This is hardly unique to Bell or Christian history. Nonetheless, it had a profound effect on the lives of many American evangelicals for whom the focus had previously been on the death of Christ on the cross as a sacrifice for sin, which functions primarily as a transaction allowing sinners to enter heaven rather than as a catalyst for new life. As one young evangelical who had gone on to start his own church explained, "Bell introduced me to a whole new way of looking at my faith. Faith was no longer about getting people to heaven, but about exploring the radical implication of the kingdom of God in this world."

Bell's "repainting of the faith" simply shattered the idea that the here and now is meant to be a time of "waiting," or pining for heaven. As Bell's world went from black and white to color, his followers felt the same freedom to view their work in the world as central to God's plan of salvation. Suddenly, every action had spiritual implications—doing work, in whatever form, when done in the spirit of what is good and true, was God's work in the world.

This kingdom-centered focus was further underscored in Bell's "repainting" of Christian soteriology. Bell believes heaven and hell are certainly real, but he also believes the promises of God are retroactive, and the distance between heaven and earth and their overlapping dimensions make what one does in this world "matter for the next." The story of the wedding of heaven and earth came into the evangelical community as something radically new and revolutionary. In the process, Bell found himself labeled a heretic.

The final notion Bell emphasized, which he derived from the Sermon on the Mount, is that blessedness is not a matter of prosperity, worldly power, or even bodily health but a state of being promised by God. This form of blessedness—expressed by Jesus' beatitude, "Blessed are the poor in spirit" (Matt 5:3), exists even in the midst of poverty, powerlessness, and sickness. There is no condition on this sacred state. There is no way to achieve it; there is no way to lose it. God, in Jesus Christ, promises that the kingdom of God dwells with all of us—even in the midst of the difficulties and sufferings of life. While not a radically new idea, the notion runs counter to the world in which Joel Osteen and others promise prosperity and tend to ignore the ever present reality of suffering. Bell makes this counter-cultural theme central to his ministry. Striving and worrying waste our energy and are precisely the opposite of the kind "non-anxious" presence that Jesus speaks about when he says, "Do not worry" (Matt 6:25).

This impulse is coincides with Bell's interest in contemplative prayer. He worked off and on with a spiritual director during his tenure at Mars Hill and spoke often of the importance of "entrusting to God" the results of one's work and efforts. In many ways, his move to Hollywood becomes a logical extension of letting go of his creation and control of Mars Hill, and a willingness to take a risk on the new and as yet undeveloped ground of his next work. But Bell remains fascinated by the way "Jesus surrendered things on the front end and entrusted the results to God."[12] Bell sees that it freed Jesus to move, and in a sense, this confirmed in Bell the idea that he no longer needs to control the consequences of his work or words.

Throughout each new or reconceived gospel idea that Bell introduced to the evangelical world, he encouraged the exploration of one's own gifts: whether music, science, literature, art, or creative expression in whatever medium. In films, sermons, music, and books, Bell himself continually introduced this intention: Aesthetics express one's deep, inner, divine designs. They motivate human beings to experience the full panoply of God's divine order and purpose in the world. This divine overflowing marks Bell's past and lays out a trajectory for his future.

---

12 Interview with Rob Bell by author, March 28, 2012.

Is Bell a Spiritual Virtuoso?

In religious scholarship, spiritual virtuosos are often compared to spiritual charismatics—talented leaders who gather a following and create religious movements, for good and for ill. Charismatics most often share the following characteristics:

- high energy, confidence, and personal authority;
- poise mixed with empathy, projecting solutions for problems;
- challengers of religious traditions, rules, and routines;
- isolation from social systems of accountability;
- hedonistic—seek creature comforts, financial success, and sometimes sexual liaisons;
- demand and need a following, without expressing the need;
- this-worldly, interested in changing and renewing the present world;
- unwilling to embrace martyrdom;
- followers are attached to person over principles (will forgive a leader's moral faults);
- social movement leaders, organizationally entrenched.

On the other hand, spiritual virtuosos embody these qualities:

- inner personal authority;
- confidence mixed with vulnerability;
- willingness to break with religious customs for the sake of spiritual and moral principles;
- detachment from, though not a rejection of, social structures;
- ascetic—practicing self-denial relative to physical and sexual needs;
- little interest in gaining followers, or creating a social movement;

- focused on personal salvation and more other-worldly;
- willingness to embrace martyrdom;
- followers are attached to principles over person (less forgiving of a leader's faults);
- authentic humility and openness.[13]

Rob Bell is an interesting mix of these characteristics. A clearly charismatic individual, he maintains a sense of personal authority and a seemingly unending sense of confidence in his own abilities. Most experience him as empathetic towards their problems and as one who projects solutions to and for them, even as he has worked through these issues. He is vulnerable at times, though his verbal acuity is so overwhelming that any issues seem to resolve as he shares them. He is quite willing and even anxious to break with custom and resist the expectations of religious rituals and traditions, even as he uses what he would call the core traditions of Baptism and Holy Communion as anchors for his liturgical and theological innovations.

Bell has consistently stepped away from bureaucratic accountability structures, though he's been willing to consult close friends and associates to receive feedback to shape his work and ministry. He's gone back and forth between self-denial and enjoying the fruits of his labors—and since 2008 he is more interested and willing to pursue the latter. His disinterest in routine and bureaucratic organizational forms led to many frustrations among those with whom he worked and served. In researching this book, I never came across one hint of sexual or moral scandal.

When I asked Bell what it's like to hear people talk about how he changed their lives, he told me that he has "had thousands of people tell me how something I've done or said had radically transformed

---

13 I was helped considerably in this list by Douglas Madsen and Peter Snow's *Charismatic Bond: Political Behavior in Time of Crisis.* Cambridge, MA: Harvard University Press, 1996. I was also informed by conversations with Steve Pfaff and Marion Goldman; the latter is author of *The American Soul Rush: Esalen and the Rise of Spiritual Privilege.* NY: New York University Press, 2012.

them." He seemed neither unappreciative nor boastful but was instead more matter of fact when he said this.[14]

There is little doubt Bell has always wanted a following. He has an intense ambition to make a difference and to share his message, but he is deeply ambivalent about the organizational side of his ministry, and, particularly more recently, less committed to sustaining a religious movement per se. In fact, Bell's interest in creating a social movement seems to have come to an end. When asked, "Would you become a megachurch pastor again?" he exclaimed with finality, "No way." The sheer magnitude of planning large events every week had clearly taken their toll.

To be sure, no one goes to Hollywood to withdraw from the world or to ignore their followers. At the same time, he rarely appeals to his wider audience through social networking and can be quite difficult to contact. This mixture of isolation and social connection has produced an effective sense of exclusivity and a still dedicated group of adherents.

So, is he a spiritual virtuoso? One expects a spiritual virtuoso to care more about his internal dialogue with spirit and much less about how he communicates with an audience. One also anticipates a sense of prayer that resonates with a transcendental intention and less with the discursive quality of his thinking about spiritual issues. With Bell, even with sermons illuminating powerful spiritual themes, his public prayers often felt like placeholders for the content to come. Indeed, he seems much more affectively present when he communicates in larger crowds than when he is one on one or with smaller groups, more of communicator of spiritual information aimed at transforming the hearer.

In this sense he embodies aspects of the virtuoso and the charismatic, but seems most fully himself as a performance artist, communicating a form of Jesus mysticism in contexts where he can express his thinking and then withdraws. Since his future is less about creating social movements than about sharing his spiritual findings, he

---

14 Interview with Rob Bell by author, March 28, 2012

finds his greatest personal solace in venues where his responsibility is to his creative comrades, an audience, and finally, and clearly most importantly, to his family.

A Harbinger of the American Christian Future?

In the American religious landscape, fewer people believe that Christianity is the only way; fewer attend church; there is a greater diversity of religious expression; and most importantly, the fastest growing subset of American people are those who claim "no religion."[15] Even so, those who claim "no religion" often still purport to believe in God and even pray frequently. We are entering a distinct phase of religious expression—one that is actively engaged in reconciling the pluralism of faith expressions and more interested in spirituality than in religious systems of belief. The American people are certainly more suspicious of those who make absolute claims about religious truth.

In this context Bell has molded a type of faith that appeals to the "not-religious-but-spiritual" ethos of the time: a faith and spiritual perspective that rings with a sense of purpose and clarity about Jesus and his way, but also focuses on the actions of charity and love over dogma and doctrine. For Bell truth is not found in belief but in lived faith that exemplifies forms of goodness, love, and beauty. Jesus incarnates and is the source of these virtues. The quality of Bell's pitch lessens the particularity of his faith and allows hearers to ask questions, pursue doubt, and try out his thinking before they commit. Bell's performance paves the way for "cultured despisers" of Christianity to take a look, and "taste" the spirit that he tries to communicate.

In this way, Bell is a postmodern evangelist—a slam poet, Billy Graham type, who beguiles with words, images, and ideas about a beautiful Jesus, whose stories transfix and transduce words into flesh, making incarnation the arbiter of all value.

---

15 See Mark Chaves' *American Religion: Contemporary Trends.*

A figure whom I think most accurately expresses and actually coincides with many of Bell's thoughts is Giano Vattimo,[16] an Italian philosopher, who argues, "By recovering the message of charity, it allows for the lightening of the dogmatic burden and a new spirit of ecumenism to fill the church. . . . Now it is time for Christianity to realize this nonreligious destiny, which is its own."[17] Vattimo's complex but elegant argument is that Christianity's central message is articulated in 1 Corinthians 13:13: "And now these three remain: faith, hope and love. But the greatest of these is love." By recovering how the action of charity trumps dogmatic pronouncements of truth, Christianity can regain its revolutionary message and its core mission, not to invent a new religion but to transcend religion through the work and actions of charity.

Vattimo (whom Bell has not read) argues that Christianity introduced the world to the notion that charity is the central driving force and that it stalled precisely when the tradition became dogmatized and bureaucratized. Vattimo asserts that when "truth" is constructed as dogma, Christianity becomes a source of coercion that seeks to dominate others. Christian history is ripe with illustrations that prove this point, but the fragmented and pluralist nature of the modern world undercuts these dogmatic claims and is precisely, from Vattimo's perspective, a result of the original Christian impulse.

---

16 Gianni Vattimo is a well-known contemporary Italian thinker and philosopher who is becoming familiar in the English-speaking world through a translation of his many works by Columbia University Press. Vattimo writes in the tradition of Nietzsche and Heidegger, arguing for Christianity's contribution to contemporary culture. Vattimo assumes a postmodern anti-foundationalism and interprets Christianity as an agent of secularization and the overcoming of absolutist metaphysics—something he argues is an important move forward. In their stead, Christianity promotes a culture of charity and justice.

17 See Gianni Vattimo's "Toward a Nonreligious Christianity," in Gianni Vattimo, John D. Caputo, and Jeffrey W. Robbin's *After the Death of God.* New York: Columbia University Press, 2007, p. 46. See the review and critique of Vattimo's work in Thomas G. Guarino, "The Return of Religion in Europe? The Postmodern Christianity of Gianni Vattimo," *Logos,* Volume 14, No. 2, 15-36.

Dogma is not the point; charity is—that is, love of those who are the least of these—the orphan, the widow, and the foreigner.

Bell's own direction forms an antiphon, "I don't think the gospels are just a nice religious idea, but I actually think it's a leap forward in human consciousness—into a tribal concentric conscious culture you have this idea that tribes should be for the betterment of other tribes."[18] Organized religion can be an instrument of the revolutionary message of Christ, according to Bell, though it also is tempted to become the point of the dogmatic spear, seeking to dominate and control others. And the church, by definition, is always under this temptation: to absolutize its rules, traditions, and dogma.

Bell posits that the wider contemporary culture sometimes understands the radical nature of the Christian revelation more than the church: "I think there is a better way to read the Bible to be true to what it is. God is pulling us forward; God isn't an old idea that needs to be fixed or updated. God has actually been pulling people forward from wherever they were all along, and for many people the reason why they don't like church, in America the Christian God is actually behind; culture has actually moved forward and God's not behind culture, trying to keep up . . . [Bell is laughing at this point]."[19]

This sounds like heresy to many, but in Bell's thinking humans tend to get caught up in a God whom they can control—a God who, for him, is a figment of their imaginations. But from Bell's perspective, this isn't the God reflected in the gospels but rather a god whom people domesticate because that god patrols the boundaries in which that particular group dwells. This tribal god makes special promises to this particular tribe. This god is not the God whom Bell sees in scripture, or the God who is revealed in Jesus Christ. For Bell, the revelation of Jesus is the revelation of a God whose "center is everywhere" and who refuses to be "localized in any one place."

18 Interview with Rob Bell by author, March 28, 2012.
19 Interview with Rob Bell by author, March 28, 2012.

It may be true that many Americans are awakening to this God—the one who cannot be controlled or localized and who takes no special interest in one group over the other. Nonetheless, this universalizing notion is tough to internalize precisely because it works against the boundary-making patterns of group identity. By nature, humans seek localizing boundaries that identify who is in and who is out. But Bell's argument is that Jesus' central revelation is of a God who is on all sides, all the time. Often critiqued as a gauzy type of liberal toleration, on this point we return to Vattimo, who states, "By saying this, I am not putting forth the usual message of tolerance. Instead, I am speaking of the ideal development of human society, hence the progressive development of all rigid categories that lead to opposition, including those of property, blood, family, along with the excesses of absolutism. The truth that shall set us free is true precisely because it frees us. If it does not free us, we ought to throw it away."[20]

Christianity, according to Bell, is not one among many traditions that express the truth of this message but is the vehicle of the final destruction of religion as such—the destruction of the notion that God absolutizes one group over another. For Bell, Christ's revelation works against this kind of boundary keeping and makes revolutionary demands on the human race to be in charity towards all— no matter their race, creed, class, tribe, gender, or sexual orientation. This high calling can easily be distorted and defamed by critics who argue, "Christ came for those of us who believe in a certain way, a certain truth, a specific group." Aware that this kind of parochialism will always be with us, Bell consistently challenges the church to avoid leading a close-minded brigade.

At the same time, Bell is not eager to force anyone to his way of thinking. He has been more than cautious about *not* arguing that his way is the *only* way. And yet he is not a relativist in the sense that anything goes, he simply claims that people have different needs and that to force them to move into frames of thought that are either not

20 See Gianni Vattimo's "Toward a Nonreligious Christianity," p. 45.

153

helpful or that they aren't prepared to embrace is, in fact, destructive. In this sense, "the later Bell" has become much less anxious about expecting people to conform to his vision and much more accepting and even indifferent to the response of others. This is, in part, a result also of Bell's disinterest in creating a movement or becoming a movement leader. As he would say, "This just isn't interesting to me."

Nevertheless, Bell represents a shift in American Christianity (and in American culture more broadly) toward what Vattimo has called a "nonreligious form of Christianity." Whether Bell describes himself as a movement leader or not, his faith acts as a clarion call for this vision. To be sure, the movement is represented in people who are currently more outside the church than in its midst, but he continues to urge the role of the church as a catalyst for this vision.

The gospel can't be protected; neither can it be destroyed or confiscated. In Bell's vision, it is always and forever revealing itself in actions of charity whether inside or outside the church. No one owns charity or the revelation of Jesus Christ. He maintains, however, that it can be distorted by dogma and obscured by those who seek to own it. He desires to witness to what he calls "the beautiful Jesus" who comes to announce the kingdom of God—where charity lives, forgiveness is practiced, and the outsider is welcomed because the outsider is the one in whom Christ dwells eternally.

The genius of Bell's message and the truth of this beautiful Jesus becomes real only when Jesus is enfleshed in acts of charity and compassion. While Christian belief is that Jesus was incarnated in flesh, this belief is all too often debated and argued to the point where tribes form, enemies are made, and the very basis of the revelation is defeated. This is precisely what Bell warns his followers against in his last Mars Hill sermon: "Beware of those who take the flesh and want to turn it back into words." Bell comforts his church and challenges them to show in actions rather than defend in words the love and truth of Jesus Christ:

i write this to you because of how many of you have been
challenged about your participation in the life of this
church, often with the accusation: but what do they believe
over there at mars hill?
as if belief, getting the words right, is the highest form of
faith. Jesus came to give us life. a living, breathing, throbbing,
pulsating blow your hair back tingle your spine roll the
windows down and drive fast experience of God right
here, right now.
word taking on flesh and blood.
and so you've found yourself defending and explaining
and trying to find the words for your experience that is
fundamentally about a reality that is beyond and more than
words.
so when you find yourselves tied up in knots, having
long discussions about who believes what, a bit like
dogs doing that sniff circle when they meet on the sidewalk,
do this:
take out a cup
and some bread
and put it in the middle of the table,
and say a prayer and examine yourselves
and then make sure everybody's rent is paid and there's
food in their fridge and clothes on their backs
and then invite everybody to say
'yes' to the resurrected Christ with whatever 'yes' they
can muster in the moment and then you take that bread
and you dip it in that cup in the ancient/future hope and
trust that there is a new creation bursting forth right here
right now and
then together taste that new life and liberation and
forgiveness and as you look those people in the eyes gathered
around that table from all walks of life and you see the new
humanity, sinners saved by grace, beggars who have
found bread showing the others beggars where they found it
remind yourselves that
this

is
what
you
believe.
remember, the movement is word to flesh.
beware of those who will take the flesh and want to turn it
back into words.[21]

In the end, the only true test of a faith begins and ends in an incarnation—love made real through actions. All else is straw.

21 Sermon, "Rob Bell's Parting Epistle to Mars Hill: "Grace + Peace,"" 12.19.2011. In *Sojourners: Faith in Action for Social Justice,* Cathleen Falsani. http:// sojo.net/blogs/2011/12/19/rob-bells-parting-epistle-mars-hill-grace-peace. The idiosyncratic use of capitalization and grammatical punctuations are original to Bell's sermon script.

ACKNOWLEDGEMENTS

Rob Bell said in his final sermon at Mars Hill, "beware of those who take the flesh and want to turn it back into words." By this Bell meant the love and beauty of Christ incarnate should mark Christian faith; otherwise the truth becomes an abstraction and the word loses its power. When I was asked to write a book on Rob Bell, I knew little about him, but my sense was that he had made something beautiful of the gospel and that he had moved beyond the usual battles between evangelicals and liberals. In my research and time with him, I found this to be true. He has done something quite remarkable, and this book has been the story of what I found. I think it will be of interest to many—those in the church and those outside it; those deeply invested in Christianity and those on its margins; those who are spiritual but not religious; those who love the church and those who don't. It's an extraordinary American story of a religious entrepreneur who made something out of nothing and did it multiple times. Bell continues to do this, and in this way he does what he preaches: his words become flesh.

I want to thank Lil Copan, my editor at Abingdon Press, who asked me to write this book and whose edits sharpened it to a fine point. I was fortunate to have many students, friends, and colleagues who gave me feedback and comments on the book, some of which I have incorporated. Any remaining errors in the book are my own. My students were helpful and leavening: Brad King, Katie Corcoran, Timothy Litts, Maya Trachtenberg, Maren Haynes, Bria Best,

Daniel Brusser, Keith Cantu, Keeli Erb, Jordan Gallivan, Jessica Lane, Rebecca Morse, Laura Randall, Brenda Serrano, Kate Stockly-Meyerdirk, David Safina, Damon Yeutter, Caitlin Wasley, Rachel Weiler and Max Yancy. My colleagues and friends were more than generous in their advice and input: James Felak, Jason Wollschleger, Kurt Johns, Bill Harper, Philip Lindholm, Steve Pfaff, Marion Goldman, Gerardo Marti and Michael Lindsay.

The book would not have been the same without Rob Bell's cooperation, nor without the thoughtful contributions of his associates and friends at Mars Hill Bible Church.

A special thank you for the encouragement and conversations with my brother, Phil Wellman, whose wisdom and enthusiasm for the project buoyed me. As always, my family is my treasure and my home. I give thanks, daily, for Annette, Constance, and Georgia—no man could be so blessed.